T0325416

THIS IS YOUR **PASSBOOK**® FOR ...

YOUTH DEVELOPMENT SPECIALIST

NATIONAL LEARNING CORPORATION®
passbooks.com

PASSBOOK® SERIES

THE *PASSBOOK® SERIES* has been created to prepare applicants and candidates for the ultimate academic battlefield – the examination room.

At some time in our lives, each and every one of us may be required to take an examination – for validation, matriculation, admission, qualification, registration, certification, or licensure.

Based on the assumption that every applicant or candidate has met the basic formal educational standards, has taken the required number of courses, and read the necessary texts, the *PASSBOOK® SERIES* furnishes the one special preparation which may assure passing with confidence, instead of failing with insecurity. Examination questions – together with answers – are furnished as the basic vehicle for study so that the mysteries of the examination and its compounding difficulties may be eliminated or diminished by a sure method.

This book is meant to help you pass your examination provided that you qualify and are serious in your objective.

The entire field is reviewed through the huge store of content information which is succinctly presented through a provocative and challenging approach – the question-and-answer method.

A climate of success is established by furnishing the correct answers at the end of each test.

You soon learn to recognize types of questions, forms of questions, and patterns of questioning. You may even begin to anticipate expected outcomes.

You perceive that many questions are repeated or adapted so that you can gain acute insights, which may enable you to score many sure points.

You learn how to confront new questions, or types of questions, and to attack them confidently and work out the correct answers.

You note objectives and emphases, and recognize pitfalls and dangers, so that you may make positive educational adjustments.

Moreover, you are kept fully informed in relation to new concepts, methods, practices, and directions in the field.

You discover that you arre actually taking the examination all the time: you are preparing for the examination by "taking" an examination, not by reading extraneous and/or supererogatory textbooks.

In short, this PASSBOOK®, used directedly, should be an important factor in helping you to pass your test.

YOUTH DEVELOPMENT SPECIALIST

DUTIES

Youth Development Specialists under supervision, and with limited latitude for the exercise of independent judgment and initiative, work as part of an interdisciplinary team to provide secure, safe care, and skill-based therapeutic interventions for pre-adjudicated and post-adjudicated youth in juvenile detention facilities and other ACS operated or managed juvenile justice facilities and programs. Youth Development Specialists facilitate youth learning of pro-social, academic, and vocational skills; mentor and guide youth individually and in groups; use a behavior management system to shape youth behavior, and encourage youth as they develop; encourage youth and family communication; build rapport with families to help them with their children; advocate for youth and their families; facilitate youth group meetings in the residential unit and elsewhere; address conflicts with crisis intervention methods such as verbal de-escalation, reframing strategies, and physical de-escalation techniques, using the least amount of physical intervention necessary; may serve as part of a rapid response team to respond to emergency situations; work with youth gangs and provide remediation activities; provide anti-bullying and violence reduction intervention; assist in the development of individualized and group treatment, programming, and safety plans; provide supervision, structure and guidance to youth, in all settings, follow all health protocols and safety and security protocols such as those concerning searches, headcounts, bed checks, intervention in volatile situations, the use of restraints, and others; conduct searches, establish ground rules and maintain protocols for the residential unit; reinforce youth behavior to support safety protocols, and assess youth's needs and risks and develop individualized safety plans; work with teachers and youth to support youth academic achievement; facilitate, engage and support youth in all activities, including school, wake-up and bedtime routines, meals, chores, recreation, religious services, court preparation, court attendance, family visits, health care visits and other activities as necessary; observe youth closely and record observations; complete required reports on attendance, incidents, and behavior observations; participate in youth admission and orientation processes; provide feedback to supervisors and managers to improve policies and procedures and complete special projects, as needed; may accompany youth to court appearances and allay youth's anxieties; drive transport vehicles and ensure youth safety in vehicles and court detention rooms; apply mechanical restraints during transport, in court detention rooms and in emergency situations as necessary. All Youth Development Specialists perform related work.

SCOPE OF THE EXAMINATION

The test may include questions requiring the use of any of the following abilities:

1. **Written Comprehension**: The ability to understand written words and paragraphs. Example: A Youth Development Specialist interprets and understands documents detailing policies, procedures and mental health care plans.
2. **Information Ordering**: The ability to follow correctly a rule or set of rules or actions in a certain order. The rule or set of rules must be given. The things or actions to be put in order can include numbers, letters, words, pictures, procedures, sentences and mathematical or logical operations. Example: A Youth Development Specialist coordinates the movement of residents during fire drills in a specific order/location based on which dorm/hall the resident occupies.

3. **Monitoring**: Monitoring/assessing performance of oneself, other individuals or organizations to make improvements or take corrective action; overseeing the quality of performance. Example: A Youth Development Specialist develops methods that allow residents and fellow staff members to accomplish daily tasks more effectively.

4. **Conflict Resolution**: Negotiating with others to resolve grievances or conflicts and handle complaints by developing a constructive solution. Example: A Youth Development Specialist prevents residents from causing harm to themselves or others and mediates various types of conflicts in order to minimize the likelihood of further altercations.

5. **Teamwork**: Developing mutual trust and cooperation while working together toward the accomplishment of a common goal or outcome. Example: A Youth Development Specialist builds a cooperative relationship with residents based on mutual trust and encourages task completion by promoting rewards.

6. **Written Expression**: The ability to use English words or sentences in writing so that others will understand. Example: A Youth Development Specialist interprets and understands documents detailing policies, procedures and mental health care plans.

7. **Problem Sensitivity**: The ability to tell when something is wrong or likely to go wrong. It includes being able to identify the whole problem, as well as elements of the problem. Example: A Youth Development Specialist recognizes oppositional/questionable body language such as gang sign calls and attitude changes.

HOW TO TAKE A TEST

I. YOU MUST PASS AN EXAMINATION

A. *WHAT EVERY CANDIDATE SHOULD KNOW*

Examination applicants often ask us for help in preparing for the written test. What can I study in advance? What kinds of questions will be asked? How will the test be given? How will the papers be graded?

As an applicant for a civil service examination, you may be wondering about some of these things. Our purpose here is to suggest effective methods of advance study and to describe civil service examinations.

Your chances for success on this examination can be increased if you know how to prepare. Those "pre-examination jitters" can be reduced if you know what to expect. You can even experience an adventure in good citizenship if you know why civil service exams are given.

B. *WHY ARE CIVIL SERVICE EXAMINATIONS GIVEN?*

Civil service examinations are important to you in two ways. As a citizen, you want public jobs filled by employees who know how to do their work. As a job seeker, you want a fair chance to compete for that job on an equal footing with other candidates. The best-known means of accomplishing this two-fold goal is the competitive examination.

Exams are widely publicized throughout the nation. They may be administered for jobs in federal, state, city, municipal, town or village governments or agencies.

Any citizen may apply, with some limitations, such as the age or residence of applicants. Your experience and education may be reviewed to see whether you meet the requirements for the particular examination. When these requirements exist, they are reasonable and applied consistently to all applicants. Thus, a competitive examination may cause you some uneasiness now, but it is your privilege and safeguard.

C. *HOW ARE CIVIL SERVICE EXAMS DEVELOPED?*

Examinations are carefully written by trained technicians who are specialists in the field known as "psychological measurement," in consultation with recognized authorities in the field of work that the test will cover. These experts recommend the subject matter areas or skills to be tested; only those knowledges or skills important to your success on the job are included. The most reliable books and source materials available are used as references. Together, the experts and technicians judge the difficulty level of the questions.

Test technicians know how to phrase questions so that the problem is clearly stated. Their ethics do not permit "trick" or "catch" questions. Questions may have been tried out on sample groups, or subjected to statistical analysis, to determine their usefulness.

Written tests are often used in combination with performance tests, ratings of training and experience, and oral interviews. All of these measures combine to form the best-known means of finding the right person for the right job.

II. HOW TO PASS THE WRITTEN TEST

A. NATURE OF THE EXAMINATION

To prepare intelligently for civil service examinations, you should know how they differ from school examinations you have taken. In school you were assigned certain definite pages to read or subjects to cover. The examination questions were quite detailed and usually emphasized memory. Civil service exams, on the other hand, try to discover your present ability to perform the duties of a position, plus your potentiality to learn these duties. In other words, a civil service exam attempts to predict how successful you will be. Questions cover such a broad area that they cannot be as minute and detailed as school exam questions.

In the public service similar kinds of work, or positions, are grouped together in one "class." This process is known as *position-classification*. All the positions in a class are paid according to the salary range for that class. One class title covers all of these positions, and they are all tested by the same examination.

B. FOUR BASIC STEPS

1) Study the announcement

How, then, can you know what subjects to study? Our best answer is: "Learn as much as possible about the class of positions for which you've applied." The exam will test the knowledge, skills and abilities needed to do the work.

Your most valuable source of information about the position you want is the official exam announcement. This announcement lists the training and experience qualifications. Check these standards and apply only if you come reasonably close to meeting them.

The brief description of the position in the examination announcement offers some clues to the subjects which will be tested. Think about the job itself. Review the duties in your mind. Can you perform them, or are there some in which you are rusty? Fill in the blank spots in your preparation.

Many jurisdictions preview the written test in the exam announcement by including a section called "Knowledge and Abilities Required," "Scope of the Examination," or some similar heading. Here you will find out specifically what fields will be tested.

2) Review your own background

Once you learn in general what the position is all about, and what you need to know to do the work, ask yourself which subjects you already know fairly well and which need improvement. You may wonder whether to concentrate on improving your strong areas or on building some background in your fields of weakness. When the announcement has specified "some knowledge" or "considerable knowledge," or has used adjectives like "beginning principles of…" or "advanced … methods," you can get a clue as to the number and difficulty of questions to be asked in any given field. More questions, and hence broader coverage, would be included for those subjects which are more important in the work. Now weigh your strengths and weaknesses against the job requirements and prepare accordingly.

3) Determine the level of the position

Another way to tell how intensively you should prepare is to understand the level of the job for which you are applying. Is it the entering level? In other words, is this the position in which beginners in a field of work are hired? Or is it an intermediate or advanced level? Sometimes this is indicated by such words as "Junior" or "Senior" in the class title. Other jurisdictions use Roman numerals to designate the level – Clerk I, Clerk II, for example. The word "Supervisor" sometimes appears in the title. If the level is not indicated by the title, check the description of duties. Will you be working under very close supervision, or will you have responsibility for independent decisions in this work?

4) Choose appropriate study materials

Now that you know the subjects to be examined and the relative amount of each subject to be covered, you can choose suitable study materials. For beginning level jobs, or even advanced ones, if you have a pronounced weakness in some aspect of your training, read a modern, standard textbook in that field. Be sure it is up to date and has general coverage. Such books are normally available at your library, and the librarian will be glad to help you locate one. For entry-level positions, questions of appropriate difficulty are chosen – neither highly advanced questions, nor those too simple. Such questions require careful thought but not advanced training.

If the position for which you are applying is technical or advanced, you will read more advanced, specialized material. If you are already familiar with the basic principles of your field, elementary textbooks would waste your time. Concentrate on advanced textbooks and technical periodicals. Think through the concepts and review difficult problems in your field.

These are all general sources. You can get more ideas on your own initiative, following these leads. For example, training manuals and publications of the government agency which employs workers in your field can be useful, particularly for technical and professional positions. A letter or visit to the government department involved may result in more specific study suggestions, and certainly will provide you with a more definite idea of the exact nature of the position you are seeking.

III. KINDS OF TESTS

Tests are used for purposes other than measuring knowledge and ability to perform specified duties. For some positions, it is equally important to test ability to make adjustments to new situations or to profit from training. In others, basic mental abilities not dependent on information are essential. Questions which test these things may not appear as pertinent to the duties of the position as those which test for knowledge and information. Yet they are often highly important parts of a fair examination. For very general questions, it is almost impossible to help you direct your study efforts. What we can do is to point out some of the more common of these general abilities needed in public service positions and describe some typical questions.

1) General information

Broad, general information has been found useful for predicting job success in some kinds of work. This is tested in a variety of ways, from vocabulary lists to questions about current events. Basic background in some field of work, such as sociology or economics, may be sampled in a group of questions. Often these are principles which have become familiar to most persons through exposure rather than through formal training. It is difficult to advise you how to study for these questions; being alert to the world around you is our best suggestion.

2) Verbal ability

An example of an ability needed in many positions is verbal or language ability. Verbal ability is, in brief, the ability to use and understand words. Vocabulary and grammar tests are typical measures of this ability. Reading comprehension or paragraph interpretation questions are common in many kinds of civil service tests. You are given a paragraph of written material and asked to find its central meaning.

3) Numerical ability

Number skills can be tested by the familiar arithmetic problem, by checking paired lists of numbers to see which are alike and which are different, or by interpreting charts and graphs. In the latter test, a graph may be printed in the test booklet which you are asked to use as the basis for answering questions.

4) Observation

A popular test for law-enforcement positions is the observation test. A picture is shown to you for several minutes, then taken away. Questions about the picture test your ability to observe both details and larger elements.

5) Following directions

In many positions in the public service, the employee must be able to carry out written instructions dependably and accurately. You may be given a chart with several columns, each column listing a variety of information. The questions require you to carry out directions involving the information given in the chart.

6) Skills and aptitudes

Performance tests effectively measure some manual skills and aptitudes. When the skill is one in which you are trained, such as typing or shorthand, you can practice. These tests are often very much like those given in business school or high school courses. For many of the other skills and aptitudes, however, no short-time preparation can be made. Skills and abilities natural to you or that you have developed throughout your lifetime are being tested.

Many of the general questions just described provide all the data needed to answer the questions and ask you to use your reasoning ability to find the answers. Your best preparation for these tests, as well as for tests of facts and ideas, is to be at your physical and mental best. You, no doubt, have your own methods of getting into an exam-taking mood and keeping "in shape." The next section lists some ideas on this subject.

IV. KINDS OF QUESTIONS

Only rarely is the "essay" question, which you answer in narrative form, used in civil service tests. Civil service tests are usually of the short-answer type. Full instructions for answering these questions will be given to you at the examination. But in case this is your first experience with short-answer questions and separate answer sheets, here is what you need to know:

1) Multiple-choice Questions

Most popular of the short-answer questions is the "multiple choice" or "best answer" question. It can be used, for example, to test for factual knowledge, ability to solve problems or judgment in meeting situations found at work.

A multiple-choice question is normally one of three types—

- It can begin with an incomplete statement followed by several possible endings. You are to find the one ending which *best* completes the statement, although some of the others may not be entirely wrong.
- It can also be a complete statement in the form of a question which is answered by choosing one of the statements listed.
- It can be in the form of a problem – again you select the best answer.

Here is an example of a multiple-choice question with a discussion which should give you some clues as to the method for choosing the right answer:

When an employee has a complaint about his assignment, the action which will *best* help him overcome his difficulty is to
- A. discuss his difficulty with his coworkers
- B. take the problem to the head of the organization
- C. take the problem to the person who gave him the assignment
- D. say nothing to anyone about his complaint

In answering this question, you should study each of the choices to find which is best. Consider choice "A" – Certainly an employee may discuss his complaint with fellow employees, but no change or improvement can result, and the complaint remains unresolved. Choice "B" is a poor choice since the head of the organization probably does not know what assignment you have been given, and taking your problem to him is known as "going over the head" of the supervisor. The supervisor, or person who made the assignment, is the person who can clarify it or correct any injustice. Choice "C" is, therefore, correct. To say nothing, as in choice "D," is unwise. Supervisors have and interest in knowing the problems employees are facing, and the employee is seeking a solution to his problem.

2) True/False Questions

The "true/false" or "right/wrong" form of question is sometimes used. Here a complete statement is given. Your job is to decide whether the statement is right or wrong.

SAMPLE: A roaming cell-phone call to a nearby city costs less than a non-roaming call to a distant city.

This statement is wrong, or false, since roaming calls are more expensive.
This is not a complete list of all possible question forms, although most of the others are variations of these common types. You will always get complete directions for

answering questions. Be sure you understand *how* to mark your answers – ask questions until you do.

V. RECORDING YOUR ANSWERS

Computer terminals are used more and more today for many different kinds of exams.

For an examination with very few applicants, you may be told to record your answers in the test booklet itself. Separate answer sheets are much more common. If this separate answer sheet is to be scored by machine – and this is often the case – it is highly important that you mark your answers correctly in order to get credit.

An electronic scoring machine is often used in civil service offices because of the speed with which papers can be scored. Machine-scored answer sheets must be marked with a pencil, which will be given to you. This pencil has a high graphite content which responds to the electronic scoring machine. As a matter of fact, stray dots may register as answers, so do not let your pencil rest on the answer sheet while you are pondering the correct answer. Also, if your pencil lead breaks or is otherwise defective, ask for another.

Since the answer sheet will be dropped in a slot in the scoring machine, be careful not to bend the corners or get the paper crumpled.

The answer sheet normally has five vertical columns of numbers, with 30 numbers to a column. These numbers correspond to the question numbers in your test booklet. After each number, going across the page are four or five pairs of dotted lines. These short dotted lines have small letters or numbers above them. The first two pairs may also have a "T" or "F" above the letters. This indicates that the first two pairs only are to be used if the questions are of the true-false type. If the questions are multiple choice, disregard the "T" and "F" and pay attention only to the small letters or numbers.

Answer your questions in the manner of the sample that follows:

32. The largest city in the United States is
    A. Washington, D.C.
    B. New York City
    C. Chicago
    D. Detroit
    E. San Francisco

1) Choose the answer you think is best. (New York City is the largest, so "B" is correct.)
2) Find the row of dotted lines numbered the same as the question you are answering. (Find row number 32)
3) Find the pair of dotted lines corresponding to the answer. (Find the pair of lines under the mark "B.")
4) Make a solid black mark between the dotted lines.

VI. BEFORE THE TEST

Common sense will help you find procedures to follow to get ready for an examination. Too many of us, however, overlook these sensible measures. Indeed, nervousness and fatigue have been found to be the most serious reasons why applicants fail to do their best on civil service tests. Here is a list of reminders:

- Begin your preparation early – Don't wait until the last minute to go scurrying around for books and materials or to find out what the position is all about.
- Prepare continuously – An hour a night for a week is better than an all-night cram session. This has been definitely established. What is more, a night a week for a month will return better dividends than crowding your study into a shorter period of time.
- Locate the place of the exam – You have been sent a notice telling you when and where to report for the examination. If the location is in a different town or otherwise unfamiliar to you, it would be well to inquire the best route and learn something about the building.
- Relax the night before the test – Allow your mind to rest. Do not study at all that night. Plan some mild recreation or diversion; then go to bed early and get a good night's sleep.
- Get up early enough to make a leisurely trip to the place for the test – This way unforeseen events, traffic snarls, unfamiliar buildings, etc. will not upset you.
- Dress comfortably – A written test is not a fashion show. You will be known by number and not by name, so wear something comfortable.
- Leave excess paraphernalia at home – Shopping bags and odd bundles will get in your way. You need bring only the items mentioned in the official notice you received; usually everything you need is provided. Do not bring reference books to the exam. They will only confuse those last minutes and be taken away from you when in the test room.
- Arrive somewhat ahead of time – If because of transportation schedules you must get there very early, bring a newspaper or magazine to take your mind off yourself while waiting.
- Locate the examination room – When you have found the proper room, you will be directed to the seat or part of the room where you will sit. Sometimes you are given a sheet of instructions to read while you are waiting. Do not fill out any forms until you are told to do so; just read them and be prepared.
- Relax and prepare to listen to the instructions
- If you have any physical problem that may keep you from doing your best, be sure to tell the test administrator. If you are sick or in poor health, you really cannot do your best on the exam. You can come back and take the test some other time.

VII. AT THE TEST

The day of the test is here and you have the test booklet in your hand. The temptation to get going is very strong. Caution! There is more to success than knowing the right answers. You must know how to identify your papers and understand variations in the type of short-answer question used in this particular examination. Follow these suggestions for maximum results from your efforts:

1) Cooperate with the monitor

The test administrator has a duty to create a situation in which you can be as much at ease as possible. He will give instructions, tell you when to begin, check to see that you are marking your answer sheet correctly, and so on. He is not there to guard you, although he will see that your competitors do not take unfair advantage. He wants to help you do your best.

2) Listen to all instructions

Don't jump the gun! Wait until you understand all directions. In most civil service tests you get more time than you need to answer the questions. So don't be in a hurry. Read each word of instructions until you clearly understand the meaning. Study the examples, listen to all announcements and follow directions. Ask questions if you do not understand what to do.

3) Identify your papers

Civil service exams are usually identified by number only. You will be assigned a number; you must not put your name on your test papers. Be sure to copy your number correctly. Since more than one exam may be given, copy your exact examination title.

4) Plan your time

Unless you are told that a test is a "speed" or "rate of work" test, speed itself is usually not important. Time enough to answer all the questions will be provided, but this does not mean that you have all day. An overall time limit has been set. Divide the total time (in minutes) by the number of questions to determine the approximate time you have for each question.

5) Do not linger over difficult questions

If you come across a difficult question, mark it with a paper clip (useful to have along) and come back to it when you have been through the booklet. One caution if you do this – be sure to skip a number on your answer sheet as well. Check often to be sure that you have not lost your place and that you are marking in the row numbered the same as the question you are answering.

6) Read the questions

Be sure you know what the question asks! Many capable people are unsuccessful because they failed to *read* the questions correctly.

7) Answer all questions

Unless you have been instructed that a penalty will be deducted for incorrect answers, it is better to guess than to omit a question.

8) Speed tests

It is often better NOT to guess on speed tests. It has been found that on timed tests people are tempted to spend the last few seconds before time is called in marking answers at random – without even reading them – in the hope of picking up a few extra points. To discourage this practice, the instructions may warn you that your score will be "corrected" for guessing. That is, a penalty will be applied. The incorrect answers will be deducted from the correct ones, or some other penalty formula will be used.

9) Review your answers

If you finish before time is called, go back to the questions you guessed or omitted to give them further thought. Review other answers if you have time.

10) Return your test materials

If you are ready to leave before others have finished or time is called, take ALL your materials to the monitor and leave quietly. Never take any test material with you. The monitor can discover whose papers are not complete, and taking a test booklet may be grounds for disqualification.

VIII. EXAMINATION TECHNIQUES

1) Read the general instructions carefully. These are usually printed on the first page of the exam booklet. As a rule, these instructions refer to the timing of the examination; the fact that you should not start work until the signal and must stop work at a signal, etc. If there are any *special* instructions, such as a choice of questions to be answered, make sure that you note this instruction carefully.

2) When you are ready to start work on the examination, that is as soon as the signal has been given, read the instructions to each question booklet, underline any key words or phrases, such as *least, best, outline, describe* and the like. In this way you will tend to answer as requested rather than discover on reviewing your paper that you *listed without describing*, that you selected the *worst* choice rather than the *best* choice, etc.

3) If the examination is of the objective or multiple-choice type – that is, each question will also give a series of possible answers: A, B, C or D, and you are called upon to select the best answer and write the letter next to that answer on your answer paper – it is advisable to start answering each question in turn. There may be anywhere from 50 to 100 such questions in the three or four hours allotted and you can see how much time would be taken if you read through all the questions before beginning to answer any. Furthermore, if you come across a question or group of questions which you know would be difficult to answer, it would undoubtedly affect your handling of all the other questions.

4) If the examination is of the essay type and contains but a few questions, it is a moot point as to whether you should read all the questions before starting to answer any one. Of course, if you are given a choice – say five out of seven and the like – then it is essential to read all the questions so you can eliminate the two that are most difficult. If, however, you are asked to answer all the questions, there may be danger in trying to answer the easiest one first because you may find that you will spend too much time on it. The best technique is to answer the first question, then proceed to the second, etc.

5) Time your answers. Before the exam begins, write down the time it started, then add the time allowed for the examination and write down the time it must be completed, then divide the time available somewhat as follows:

- If 3-1/2 hours are allowed, that would be 210 minutes. If you have 80 objective-type questions, that would be an average of 2-1/2 minutes per question. Allow yourself no more than 2 minutes per question, or a total of 160 minutes, which will permit about 50 minutes to review.
- If for the time allotment of 210 minutes there are 7 essay questions to answer, that would average about 30 minutes a question. Give yourself only 25 minutes per question so that you have about 35 minutes to review.

6) The most important instruction is to *read each question* and make sure you know what is wanted. The second most important instruction is to *time yourself properly* so that you answer every question. The third most important instruction is to *answer every question*. Guess if you have to but include something for each question. Remember that you will receive no credit for a blank and will probably receive some credit if you write something in answer to an essay question. If you guess a letter – say "B" for a multiple-choice question – you may have guessed right. If you leave a blank as an answer to a multiple-choice question, the examiners may respect your feelings but it will not add a point to your score. Some exams may penalize you for wrong answers, so in such cases *only*, you may not want to guess unless you have some basis for your answer.

7) Suggestions
   a. Objective-type questions
      1. Examine the question booklet for proper sequence of pages and questions
      2. Read all instructions carefully
      3. Skip any question which seems too difficult; return to it after all other questions have been answered
      4. Apportion your time properly; do not spend too much time on any single question or group of questions
      5. Note and underline key words – *all, most, fewest, least, best, worst, same, opposite,* etc.
      6. Pay particular attention to negatives
      7. Note unusual option, e.g., unduly long, short, complex, different or similar in content to the body of the question
      8. Observe the use of "hedging" words – *probably, may, most likely,* etc.
      9. Make sure that your answer is put next to the same number as the question
      10. Do not second-guess unless you have good reason to believe the second answer is definitely more correct
      11. Cross out original answer if you decide another answer is more accurate; do not erase until you are ready to hand your paper in
      12. Answer all questions; guess unless instructed otherwise
      13. Leave time for review

   b. Essay questions
      1. Read each question carefully
      2. Determine exactly what is wanted. Underline key words or phrases.
      3. Decide on outline or paragraph answer

4. Include many different points and elements unless asked to develop any one or two points or elements
5. Show impartiality by giving pros and cons unless directed to select one side only
6. Make and write down any assumptions you find necessary to answer the questions
7. Watch your English, grammar, punctuation and choice of words
8. Time your answers; don't crowd material

8) Answering the essay question

Most essay questions can be answered by framing the specific response around several key words or ideas. Here are a few such key words or ideas:

M's: manpower, materials, methods, money, management
P's: purpose, program, policy, plan, procedure, practice, problems, pitfalls, personnel, public relations
  a. Six basic steps in handling problems:
    1. Preliminary plan and background development
    2. Collect information, data and facts
    3. Analyze and interpret information, data and facts
    4. Analyze and develop solutions as well as make recommendations
    5. Prepare report and sell recommendations
    6. Install recommendations and follow up effectiveness

  b. Pitfalls to avoid
    1. *Taking things for granted* – A statement of the situation does not necessarily imply that each of the elements is necessarily true; for example, a complaint may be invalid and biased so that all that can be taken for granted is that a complaint has been registered
    2. *Considering only one side of a situation* – Wherever possible, indicate several alternatives and then point out the reasons you selected the best one
    3. *Failing to indicate follow up* – Whenever your answer indicates action on your part, make certain that you will take proper follow-up action to see how successful your recommendations, procedures or actions turn out to be
    4. *Taking too long in answering any single question* – Remember to time your answers properly

IX. AFTER THE TEST

Scoring procedures differ in detail among civil service jurisdictions although the general principles are the same. Whether the papers are hand-scored or graded by machine we have described, they are nearly always graded by number. That is, the person who marks the paper knows only the number – never the name – of the applicant. Not until all the papers have been graded will they be matched with names. If other tests, such as training and experience or oral interview ratings have been given, scores will be combined. Different parts of the examination usually have different weights. For example, the written test might count 60 percent of the final grade, and a rating of training and experience 40 percent. In many jurisdictions, veterans will have a certain number of points added to their grades.

After the final grade has been determined, the names are placed in grade order and an eligible list is established. There are various methods for resolving ties between those who get the same final grade – probably the most common is to place first the name of the person whose application was received first. Job offers are made from the eligible list in the order the names appear on it. You will be notified of your grade and your rank as soon as all these computations have been made. This will be done as rapidly as possible.

People who are found to meet the requirements in the announcement are called "eligibles." Their names are put on a list of eligible candidates. An eligible's chances of getting a job depend on how high he stands on this list and how fast agencies are filling jobs from the list.

When a job is to be filled from a list of eligibles, the agency asks for the names of people on the list of eligibles for that job. When the civil service commission receives this request, it sends to the agency the names of the three people highest on this list. Or, if the job to be filled has specialized requirements, the office sends the agency the names of the top three persons who meet these requirements from the general list.

The appointing officer makes a choice from among the three people whose names were sent to him. If the selected person accepts the appointment, the names of the others are put back on the list to be considered for future openings.

That is the rule in hiring from all kinds of eligible lists, whether they are for typist, carpenter, chemist, or something else. For every vacancy, the appointing officer has his choice of any one of the top three eligibles on the list. This explains why the person whose name is on top of the list sometimes does not get an appointment when some of the persons lower on the list do. If the appointing officer chooses the second or third eligible, the No. 1 eligible does not get a job at once, but stays on the list until he is appointed or the list is terminated.

X. HOW TO PASS THE INTERVIEW TEST

The examination for which you applied requires an oral interview test. You have already taken the written test and you are now being called for the interview test – the final part of the formal examination.

You may think that it is not possible to prepare for an interview test and that there are no procedures to follow during an interview. Our purpose is to point out some things you can do in advance that will help you and some good rules to follow and pitfalls to avoid while you are being interviewed.

What is an interview supposed to test?
The written examination is designed to test the technical knowledge and competence of the candidate; the oral is designed to evaluate intangible qualities, not readily measured otherwise, and to establish a list showing the relative fitness of each candidate – as measured against his competitors – for the position sought. Scoring is not on the basis of "right" and "wrong," but on a sliding scale of values ranging from "not passable" to "outstanding." As a matter of fact, it is possible to achieve a relatively low score without a single "incorrect" answer because of evident weakness in the qualities being measured.

Occasionally, an examination may consist entirely of an oral test – either an individual or a group oral. In such cases, information is sought concerning the technical knowledges and abilities of the candidate, since there has been no written examination for this purpose. More commonly, however, an oral test is used to supplement a written examination.

Who conducts interviews?

The composition of oral boards varies among different jurisdictions. In nearly all, a representative of the personnel department serves as chairman. One of the members of the board may be a representative of the department in which the candidate would work. In some cases, "outside experts" are used, and, frequently, a businessman or some other representative of the general public is asked to serve. Labor and management or other special groups may be represented. The aim is to secure the services of experts in the appropriate field.

However the board is composed, it is a good idea (and not at all improper or unethical) to ascertain in advance of the interview who the members are and what groups they represent. When you are introduced to them, you will have some idea of their backgrounds and interests, and at least you will not stutter and stammer over their names.

What should be done before the interview?

While knowledge about the board members is useful and takes some of the surprise element out of the interview, there is other preparation which is more substantive. It *is* possible to prepare for an oral interview – in several ways:

1) Keep a copy of your application and review it carefully before the interview

This may be the only document before the oral board, and the starting point of the interview. Know what education and experience you have listed there, and the sequence and dates of all of it. Sometimes the board will ask you to review the highlights of your experience for them; you should not have to hem and haw doing it.

2) Study the class specification and the examination announcement

Usually, the oral board has one or both of these to guide them. The qualities, characteristics or knowledges required by the position sought are stated in these documents. They offer valuable clues as to the nature of the oral interview. For example, if the job involves supervisory responsibilities, the announcement will usually indicate that knowledge of modern supervisory methods and the qualifications of the candidate as a supervisor will be tested. If so, you can expect such questions, frequently in the form of a hypothetical situation which you are expected to solve. NEVER go into an oral without knowledge of the duties and responsibilities of the job you seek.

3) Think through each qualification required

Try to visualize the kind of questions you would ask if you were a board member. How well could you answer them? Try especially to appraise your own knowledge and background in each area, *measured against the job sought*, and identify any areas in which you are weak. Be critical and realistic – do not flatter yourself.

4) Do some general reading in areas in which you feel you may be weak

For example, if the job involves supervision and your past experience has NOT, some general reading in supervisory methods and practices, particularly in the field of human relations, might be useful. Do NOT study agency procedures or detailed manuals. The oral board will be testing your understanding and capacity, not your memory.

5) Get a good night's sleep and watch your general health and mental attitude

You will want a clear head at the interview. Take care of a cold or any other minor ailment, and of course, no hangovers.

What should be done on the day of the interview?

Now comes the day of the interview itself. Give yourself plenty of time to get there. Plan to arrive somewhat ahead of the scheduled time, particularly if your appointment is in the fore part of the day. If a previous candidate fails to appear, the board might be ready for you a bit early. By early afternoon an oral board is almost invariably behind schedule if there are many candidates, and you may have to wait. Take along a book or magazine to read, or your application to review, but leave any extraneous material in the waiting room when you go in for your interview. In any event, relax and compose yourself.

The matter of dress is important. The board is forming impressions about you – from your experience, your manners, your attitude, and your appearance. Give your personal appearance careful attention. Dress your best, but not your flashiest. Choose conservative, appropriate clothing, and be sure it is immaculate. This is a business interview, and your appearance should indicate that you regard it as such. Besides, being well groomed and properly dressed will help boost your confidence.

Sooner or later, someone will call your name and escort you into the interview room. *This is it.* From here on you are on your own. It is too late for any more preparation. But remember, you asked for this opportunity to prove your fitness, and you are here because your request was granted.

What happens when you go in?

The usual sequence of events will be as follows: The clerk (who is often the board stenographer) will introduce you to the chairman of the oral board, who will introduce you to the other members of the board. Acknowledge the introductions before you sit down. Do not be surprised if you find a microphone facing you or a stenotypist sitting by. Oral interviews are usually recorded in the event of an appeal or other review.

Usually the chairman of the board will open the interview by reviewing the highlights of your education and work experience from your application – primarily for the benefit of the other members of the board, as well as to get the material into the record. Do not interrupt or comment unless there is an error or significant misinterpretation; if that is the case, do not hesitate. But do not quibble about insignificant matters. Also, he will usually ask you some question about your education, experience or your present job – partly to get you to start talking and to establish the interviewing "rapport." He may start the actual questioning, or turn it over to one of the other members. Frequently, each member undertakes the questioning on a particular area, one in which he is perhaps most competent, so you can expect each member to participate in the examination. Because time is limited, you may also expect some rather abrupt switches in the direction the questioning takes, so do not be upset by it. Normally, a board member will not pursue a single line of questioning unless he discovers a particular strength or weakness.

After each member has participated, the chairman will usually ask whether any member has any further questions, then will ask you if you have anything you wish to add. Unless you are expecting this question, it may floor you. Worse, it may start you off on an extended, extemporaneous speech. The board is not usually seeking more information. The question is principally to offer you a last opportunity to present further qualifications or to indicate that you have nothing to add. So, if you feel that a significant qualification or characteristic has been overlooked, it is proper to point it out in a sentence or so. Do not compliment the board on the thoroughness of their examination – they have been sketchy, and you know it. If you wish, merely say, "No thank you, I have nothing further to add." This is a point where you can "talk yourself out" of a good impression or fail to present an important bit of information. Remember, *you close the interview yourself.*

The chairman will then say, "That is all, Mr. _____, thank you." Do not be startled; the interview is over, and quicker than you think. Thank him, gather your belongings and take your leave. Save your sigh of relief for the other side of the door.

How to put your best foot forward

Throughout this entire process, you may feel that the board individually and collectively is trying to pierce your defenses, seek out your hidden weaknesses and embarrass and confuse you. Actually, this is not true. They are obliged to make an appraisal of your qualifications for the job you are seeking, and they want to see you in your best light. Remember, they must interview all candidates and a non-cooperative candidate may become a failure in spite of their best efforts to bring out his qualifications. Here are 15 suggestions that will help you:

1) Be natural – Keep your attitude confident, not cocky

If you are not confident that you can do the job, do not expect the board to be. Do not apologize for your weaknesses, try to bring out your strong points. The board is interested in a positive, not negative, presentation. Cockiness will antagonize any board member and make him wonder if you are covering up a weakness by a false show of strength.

2) Get comfortable, but don't lounge or sprawl

Sit erectly but not stiffly. A careless posture may lead the board to conclude that you are careless in other things, or at least that you are not impressed by the importance of the occasion. Either conclusion is natural, even if incorrect. Do not fuss with your clothing, a pencil or an ashtray. Your hands may occasionally be useful to emphasize a point; do not let them become a point of distraction.

3) Do not wisecrack or make small talk

This is a serious situation, and your attitude should show that you consider it as such. Further, the time of the board is limited – they do not want to waste it, and neither should you.

4) Do not exaggerate your experience or abilities

In the first place, from information in the application or other interviews and sources, the board may know more about you than you think. Secondly, you probably will not get away with it. An experienced board is rather adept at spotting such a situation, so do not take the chance.

5) If you know a board member, do not make a point of it, yet do not hide it

Certainly you are not fooling him, and probably not the other members of the board. Do not try to take advantage of your acquaintanceship – it will probably do you little good.

6) Do not dominate the interview

Let the board do that. They will give you the clues – do not assume that you have to do all the talking. Realize that the board has a number of questions to ask you, and do not try to take up all the interview time by showing off your extensive knowledge of the answer to the first one.

7) Be attentive

You only have 20 minutes or so, and you should keep your attention at its sharpest throughout. When a member is addressing a problem or question to you, give him your undivided attention. Address your reply principally to him, but do not exclude the other board members.

8) Do not interrupt

A board member may be stating a problem for you to analyze. He will ask you a question when the time comes. Let him state the problem, and wait for the question.

9) Make sure you understand the question

Do not try to answer until you are sure what the question is. If it is not clear, restate it in your own words or ask the board member to clarify it for you. However, do not haggle about minor elements.

10) Reply promptly but not hastily

A common entry on oral board rating sheets is "candidate responded readily," or "candidate hesitated in replies." Respond as promptly and quickly as you can, but do not jump to a hasty, ill-considered answer.

11) Do not be peremptory in your answers

A brief answer is proper – but do not fire your answer back. That is a losing game from your point of view. The board member can probably ask questions much faster than you can answer them.

12) Do not try to create the answer you think the board member wants

He is interested in what kind of mind you have and how it works – not in playing games. Furthermore, he can usually spot this practice and will actually grade you down on it.

13) Do not switch sides in your reply merely to agree with a board member

Frequently, a member will take a contrary position merely to draw you out and to see if you are willing and able to defend your point of view. Do not start a debate, yet do not surrender a good position. If a position is worth taking, it is worth defending.

14) Do not be afraid to admit an error in judgment if you are shown to be wrong

The board knows that you are forced to reply without any opportunity for careful consideration. Your answer may be demonstrably wrong. If so, admit it and get on with the interview.

15) Do not dwell at length on your present job

The opening question may relate to your present assignment. Answer the question but do not go into an extended discussion. You are being examined for a *new* job, not your present one. As a matter of fact, try to phrase ALL your answers in terms of the job for which you are being examined.

Basis of Rating

Probably you will forget most of these "do's" and "don'ts" when you walk into the oral interview room. Even remembering them all will not ensure you a passing grade. Perhaps you did not have the qualifications in the first place. But remembering them will help you to put your best foot forward, without treading on the toes of the board members.

Rumor and popular opinion to the contrary notwithstanding, an oral board wants you to make the best appearance possible. They know you are under pressure – but they also want to see how you respond to it as a guide to what your reaction would be under the pressures of the job you seek. They will be influenced by the degree of poise you display, the personal traits you show and the manner in which you respond.

ABOUT THIS BOOK

This book contains tests divided into Examination Sections. Go through each test, answering every question in the margin. At the end of each test look at the answer key and check your answers. On the ones you got wrong, look at the right answer choice and learn. Do not fill in the answers first. Do not memorize the questions and answers, but understand the answer and principles involved. On your test, the questions will likely be different from the samples. Questions are changed and new ones added. If you understand these past questions you should have success with any changes that arise. Tests may consist of several types of questions. We have additional books on each subject should more study be advisable or necessary for you. Finally, the more you study, the better prepared you will be. This book is intended to be the last thing you study before you walk into the examination room. Prior study of relevant texts is also recommended. NLC publishes some of these in our Fundamental Series. Knowledge and good sense are important factors in passing your exam. Good luck also helps. So now study this Passbook, absorb the material contained within and take that knowledge into the examination. Then do your best to pass that exam.

———

EXAMINATION SECTION

EXAMINATION SECTION
TEST 1

DIRECTIONS: Each question or incomplete statement is followed by several suggested answers or completions. Select the one that BEST answers the question or completes the statement. *PRINT THE LETTER OF THE CORRECT ANSWER IN THE SPACE AT THE RIGHT.*

1. Counselors on duty during visiting hours at detention centers are required to remain at their posts and to be very watchful until visiting hours are over. During one visiting period, the counselor on duty finds that there are few visitors and that conditions are peaceful in the visiting area.
Which of the following would be the *most appropriate* behavior for the counselor?

    A. Leave the visiting area to attend to other official duties, but check back frequently to make certain that conditions remain quiet.
    B. Remain in the visiting area and take advantage of untroubled conditions by catching up on needed report writing.
    C. Leave the visiting area to attend to other official duties, but not before arranging for a reliable visitor to summon help immediately if needed.
    D. Remain in the visiting area and pay strict attention to conditions in that area.

1.____

2. A counselor supervising a group of children in a dormitory in a detention center observes that a newly admitted child appears shy and withdrawn and generally avoids contact with the other children.
Which of the following would be the BEST action for the counselor to take?

    A. Mentally note the child's behavior and report it to the supervisor if this behavior continues
    B. Advise the child that "the only way to get along is to go along" and that his behavior may cause resentment
    C. Arrange for an older child to initiate the newly arrived child into the group's activities
    D. Ask the child to explain his behavior at the next group counseling session

2.____

3. A counselor in a dormitory observes two children fighting. Which of the following would be the BEST action for the counselor to take?

    A. Stop the fight quickly
    B. Permit the fight to continue until one child is clearly ahead
    C. Referee the fight to make sure that proper rules are followed
    D. Have one of the stronger children stop the fight

3.____

4. A counselor in a detention center finds one of the detained children by himself spraying graffiti on his dormitory walls with a spray can.
Which of the following actions by the counselor is LEAST justified?

    A. Take the spray can away from the child
    B. Have all the children in the dormitory remove the graffiti
    C. Have the child who used the spray can remove the graffiti
    D. Explain to the child who sprayed the walls why he should not have done so

4.____

5. One of the children in a group asks the counselor for permission to speak to the social   5.____
   worker on an important family matter.
   Which of the following is the BEST action for the counselor to take?

    A. Advise the child to secure the benefits of group counseling before seeing the social
          worker
       B. Refer the child to the social worker
       C. Interview the child to see if the request is really justified
       D. Explain to the child that self-reliance, and not dependence on the social worker, is
          the key to maturity

6. One of the responsibilities of a counselor on the night tour of a detention center is to   6.____
   make periodic checks of the children's sleeping quarters and observe any child with
   unusual sleeping behavior.
   If a counselor has just observed a child with unusual sleeping behavior, what should
   he do *next*?

    A. Continue his observations on succeeding checks, and, if the behavior is repeated,
          discuss it with the child
       B. Ignore this behavior if no other children in the sleeping quarters seem to be both-
          ered
       C. Get a fellow staff member to confirm the observation and then wake the child
       D. Report the observed behavior to his superior

7. A counselor in a dormitory has completed a head count of children and finds that the   7.____
   head count is one less than it should be.
   Which of the following is the *next* action the counselor should take?

    A. Immediately report the child missing
       B. Alert the child's nearest relatives and advise them not to shelter a runaway
       C. Check all areas of the dormitory to make certain the child is really missing
       D. Question the other children to learn whether they know the reason for the child's
          disappearance

8. Al, a sixteen-year-old boy, was described by psychologists as "psychopathic." Ben,   8.____
   another sixteen-year-old boy, was described by psychologists as "inhibited and conform-
   ist." Which of the following is MOST correct?

    A. Al is more likely than Ben to become delinquent.
       B. Ben is more likely than Al to become delinquent.
       C. Both boys are about equally likely to become delinquent.
       D. Neither boy is likely to become delinquent.

9. John, one of the juveniles under your supervision, admitted after questioning that he had   9.____
   beaten up Tom, another youth in the institution. John said he did it because Tom is a
   "punk."
   Of the following, the BEST action to take in response to John's statement would be to

    A. advise John to make certain that someone is a "punk" before taking any action
       B. agree that "punks" deserve to be beaten for the good of the rest of the boys
       C. question John as to why he believes Tom is a "punk" and why "punks" should be
          beaten
       D. agree reluctantly that Tom is a "punk," but emphasize that he should not have been
          beaten

10. Children in a juvenile detention center are prohibited from having in their possession items which are unlawful, which will assist them to escape, or which can be used to injure or harm others.
On the basis of this statement, which of the following items is LEAST likely to be prohibited?

    A. Wire clothes hanger
    B. Door knob with a spindle
    C. Two-foot length of garden hose
    D. Bar of soap

10.____

Questions 11-15.

DIRECTIONS: Answer Questions 11 through 15 *only* on the basis of the information and the sample report form given below.

On the evening of Wednesday, October 30, 2014, a counselor is making a routine check of Dormitory A-3 at Smith Juvenile Center. In checking the bathroom, the counselor discovers that a sink is full of water and is starting to overflow onto the floor. The cold-water tap is leaking and the sink is not draining. The counselor finds a wad of paper blocking the sink drain. When the paper is removed, the sink drains immediately. However, the cold-water tap cannot be turned off. The counselor goes to the desk and begins to fill out the following Repair Request Form. The counselor making the repair request is L. Rolin. The other counselor on duty in Dormitory A-3 is A. Pollitt. The department head for this dormitory is S. Jones.

REPAIR REQUEST FORM

A. Name of Juvenile Center _____

B. Exact location of repair job _____

C. Date _____

D. Type of condition requiring repair _____
_____

E. Signature of staff member requesting repair _____

F. Signature of department head approving _____

G. Signature of repair worker and date repair completed _____
_____ (Date) _____

---

11. The information that should be indicated on Line B of the Repair Request Form is

    A. Smith Juvenile Center   B. Dormitory A
    C. Sink, Smith Juvenile Center   D. Bathroom, Dormity A-3

11.____

12. Which of the following is the MOST *exact* and *informative* entry for Line C?

    A. Wednesday evening   B. 2014
    C. October 2011   D. October 30, 2014

12.____

13. Which of the following entries for Line D should be the *most useful* to a repair supervisor in deciding what kind of repair worker should make the repair and what equipment the worker should have?

13.____

    A.   Sink was discovered overflowing onto floor
    B.   Cold-water tap is leaking
    C.   Cold-water tap is dripping and sink is not draining
    D.   Sink drain is plugged up

14.   The person whose signature should appear on Line E is   14._____

    A.   L. Rolin   B.   A. Pollitt
    C.   S. Jones   D.   the repair worker

15.   A line on the Repair Request Form that CANNOT be filled out on the basis of the infor-   15._____
     mation given above is

    A.   line A   B.   line D   C.   line F   D.   line G

16.   Certain youngsters in a juvenile detention facility are constantly fighting with each other.   16._____
     So far no one has been seriously hurt. Another youth who lives in the same dormitory
     has complained to the counselor because he is afraid he might be involved in future out-
     breaks, possibly as a victim.
     Of the following, the BEST action for the counselor to take would be to

    A.   assure the youth who complained that he really has nothing to fear, because the
        youngsters complained about fighting only among themselves
    B.   explain to the youth who complained that fighting among adolescents is part of the
        process of "growing up," and that he should be a part of this process if he wants to
        develop normally
    C.   report the matter to his superiors, with a recommendation that the youth who com-
        plained should be transferred to another dormitory if possible
    D.   watch the situation carefully and take immediate action when someone is seriously
        hurt

17.   A fundamental responsibility of a detention facility is to provide adequate medical care for   17._____
     the juvenile remanded to it. Assume that a youth suddenly complains to a counselor of
     severe stomach pains.
     Of the following, what is the FIRST action the counselor should take?

    A.   Observe the youth for a day to see if the pains persist
    B.   Check the youth's medical history to see if he has a pattern of faking illness
    C.   Secure medical attention as soon as possible
    D.   Try to alleviate the pain with aspirin

18.   The gang, like any group, has a powerful influence in enforcing comformity on its mem-   18._____
     bers. Individual gang members hate to be considered different from their fellow gang
     members. For example, the way most members of the gang act or dress is compelling
     reason for other gang members to do the same.
     Which of the following statements BEST expresses the meaning of the above para-
     graph?

    A.   Gang members live in fear of behaving in a way contrary to gang rules
    B.   Force and violence serve to make a gang member conform to the gang way of life
    C.   Gang members behave the way they do because society is weak
    D.   The behavior of gang members is often governed by their wish to conform

19. Some experts on juvenile groups have observed that, if membership in the delinquent gang were not rewarding to the individual gang member, the gang would cease to exist. The implication of this statement is, *most nearly,* that   19.____

    A.   the threats of rival gangs serve to unify many delinquent gangs
    B.   many gangs are very unstable in membership, and the loyalty of members is low
    C.   gang membership meets the needs of some juveniles
    D.   the lives of many gang members are characterized by desperation rather than fun

20. The daytime counselor in a detention center, before going off duty, confers with the incoming nighttime counselor and discusses the behavior of the group during his day tour.   20.____
    Of the following, the MAIN reason for this conference should be to

    A.   build up a file of experiences useful for group counseling
    B.   make the juveniles aware that both counselors are in agreement
    C.   alert the oncoming counselor to daytime behavior that may be repeated at night
    D.   avoid duplication in written reports of incidents

Questions 21-25.

DIRECTIONS: Answer Questions 21 through 25 *only* on the basis of the information and the sample form given below.

When children are admitted to a juvenile detention center, all their personal property, including the clothing that they are wearing, is taken away from them. A record is kept of this property on the following Personal Property List and, when they leave the center, all their personal property is returned to them.

SAMPLE FORM FOR LISTING PERSONAL PROPERTY

PERSONAL PROPERTY LIST			
Item	Color	Material	Quantity
Shirt			
Pants			
Belt			
Undershorts			
Undershirt			
Socks			
Sneakers			
Shoes			
Sandals			
Coat			
Hat			
Sweater			
Other (describe)			
Name of Child		Admission Date	

Two children, Allen Adams and Bertram Brown, were admitted to Juvenile Center X on October 1, 2014. An admissions counselor found that they had the following items of personal property:

ALLEN ADAMS - 1 pair white cotton socks, 1 pair blue sneakers, blue cotton shirt, tan wool pants, brown vinyl belt, white cotton under-shorts, white cotton undershirt, wristwatch, brown wool sweater, and a ballpoint pen.

BERTRAM BROWN - 1 pair black cotton socks, 1 pair white sneakers, white polyester shirt, tan cotton pants, white cotton undershorts, white cotton undershirt, tan leather coat, brown plastic wallet with bus pass, and 50¢ in change.

21. Which of the following is the MOST *complete* and *correct* entry for "Shirt" on the Personal Property List for Allen Adams?   21._____

    A. White, cotton, one
    B. Blue, wool, one
    C. Blue, cotton, one
    D. White, polyester, one

22. If, at the time of admission, the child does not have with him or is not wearing one of the items listed, the line for that item is left blank.   22._____
    Which one of the following items should be left *blank* on the Personal Property List for Bertram Brown?

    A. Pants   B. Belt   C. Sneakers   D. Other

23. Which of the following is the MOST *complete* and *correct* entry for "Other" on the Personal Property List for Allen Adams?   23._____

    A. Wristwatch, one; Ballpoint pen, one
    B. Wristwatch, one; Ballpoint pen, one; Sweater, brown, wool, one
    C. Socks, white, cotton, one; Sweater, brown, wool, one
    D. Socks, white, cotton, one; Wristwatch, one; Brown sweater, wool, one

24. For which of the following items should there be NO entry on the Personal Property List either for Allen Adams or for Bertram Brown?   24._____

    A. Undershorts   B. Sneakers   C. Coat   D. Hat

25. Allen Adams and Bertram Brown have two items of personal property that are identical in kind, color, and quantity. These *two* items are   25._____

    A. Shirt; Pants
    B. Undershorts; Socks
    C. Pants; Undershorts
    D. Undershirt; Undershorts

KEY (CORRECT ANSWERS)

1.	D	11.	D
2.	A	12.	D
3.	A	13.	B
4.	B	14.	A
5.	D	15.	D
6.	C	16.	C
7.	A	17.	C
8.	C	18.	D
9.	C	19.	C
10.	D	20.	C

21. C
22. B
23. A
24. D
25. D

TEST 2

DIRECTIONS: Each question or incomplete statement is followed by several suggested answers or completions. Select the one that BEST answers the question or completes the statement. *PRINT THE LETTER OF THE CORRECT ANSWER IN THE SPACE AT THE RIGHT.*

1. The 14- and 15-year-old youths in male dormitory B have daily group meetings. During one of these meetings, the counselor helps the group to realize that they are being "fooled" and "taken advantage of" by a youth who had achieved a position of leadership in the group as a result of his bullying and his more seriously delinquent behavior. Reducing the group's respect for this youth is

    1.____

   A. *probably good,* because adolescence is an impressionable period and youths may tend to imitate a more seriously delinquent youth whom they admire
   B. *probably bad,* because a youth involved in more serious delinquency is exactly the kind of experienced leader who can be used to help the counselor keep the other youths "in line"
   C. *probably bad,* because the realization that one of their peers, whom they had trusted, was taking advantage of them will tend to make the youths feel even more anti-social
   D. *probably neither good nor bad,* since young people are not influenced very much by other youths whom they meet in the artificial environment of a detention facility

2. Of the following, the BEST reason so much research on juvenile delinquency focuses on gangs is that

    2.____

   A. juvenile delinquency is caused by gangs
   B. the elimination of gangs is very likely to eliminate delinquency among juveniles
   C. individual delinquents very often form gangs or are members of gangs
   D. the highest delinquency rates are found among boys who are aggressive and out-going

3. Juvenile delinquency shows many different forms, different degrees of intensity, and varies for many reasons.
   This statement implies, *most nearly,* that

    3.____

   A. "hard core" delinquents are admired by their peers for stealing or fighting
   B. whether or not a boy is arrested for delinquency depends in part on chance
   C. delinquents should be encouraged to reform their ways
   D. no single cause is sufficient to explain juvenile delinquency

4. State statutes limit confinement of people under 16 years of age to a maximum of 3 years, regardless of how serious the crime. In practice, relatively few delinquents under 16 are incarcerated in juvenile correction facilities. Of those incarcerated, only a handful are confined more than 15 months, and most are free in less than a year.
   This statement implies that a 14-year-old youth found delinquent by a State Juvenile Court would, *most likely,*

    4.____

   A. be confined only a few days
   B. be confined only until age 16
   C. be confined for the maximum period of time
   D. not be confined

5. Juveniles who are remanded to detention facilities often arrive distressed and angry. Some of these juveniles will look upon all counselors, teachers and other members of the detention staff with hostility and distrust.
Of the following, probably the MOST effective way a counselor can communicate genuine concern for the welfare of these detained juveniles is for the counselor to

    A. tell the juveniles frequently that he understands their problems and is concerned about their welfare
    B. appear unconcerned and wait for the juveniles to "test" his concern for them
    C. make an effort to alleviate the problems experienced by juveniles in detention
    D. "play along" with the juveniles by telling them that, although most counselors cannot be trusted, he is different and can be looked upon as a friend

5.____

6. Adolescence is a maturational phase in which the young person is trying to redefine himself. It is a period in which the adolescent is striving to throw off the shackles of childhood and become a person in his own right.
In dealing with the adolescent in a juvenile detention center, which of the following is the BEST approach for a counselor to take?

    A. Be aware that adolescent behavior in general is often inconsistent - mature one moment, immature the next.
    B. Make the detained adolescent aware that he is bad, and that everyone must strictly obey the rules.
    C. Recognize that the youthful offender is basically immature and therefore cannot be held responsible for his actions.
    D. Treat him as an equal and encourage mature behavior by allowing him to make his own interpretations of rules.

6.____

7. During the school year, the children at a juvenile detention center are expected to go to school unless excused by a doctor or for another special reason. One morning a child in a counselor's group refuses to go to school and refuses to explain why.
Of the following, the BEST action for the counselor to take *next* in this situation would be to

    A. escort the child forcibly to the classroom
    B. warn the child of the severe consequences if he persists in his refusal to go
    C. report the matter to his supervisor
    D. permit the child to have his way

7.____

8. Both individual and group counseling are used in juvenile detention centers.
Which of the following is the MOST important reason for the use of group counseling?

    A. It is more efficient for a counselor to share his knowledge with a group all at once than to talk to individuals separately.
    B. Juveniles usually will not respond well to a counselor unless the counselor is part of a group.
    C. The group session is a more direct way for the counselor to observe and deal with group behavior.
    D. Juveniles, who have not yet reached maturity, cannot benefit from individual counseling.

8.____

9. Behavioral problems impair peace and order within the institution and reinforce negative values for the juveniles themselves.
Which of the following statements about behavior problems in a juvenile detention facility is CORRECT?

    A. Runaways present a problem to group counselors because a group has difficulty in adjusting when one of its members is not present at a session.
    B. Drinking is a problem because it is in violation of a state law which prohibits drinking by persons under 21 years of age.
    C. Sexual problems can be expected to appear in an adolescent population confined in a detention facility.
    D. Behavioral problems do not usually occur among juvenile offenders when counselors have been conscientious in performing their duties.

9.____

10. The counselor must maintain a certain degree of aloofness from the children in the detention center and must maintain his image as a figure of authority.
Of the following, the BEST approach for the counselor to take in following this concept is to

    A. change rules frequently so as to keep the youths in a state of uncertainty
    B. avoid having the youths obey orders as a personal favor to him because they will then expect favors in return
    C. try to develop as many personal friendships as possible because the youths will not take advantage of a friend
    D. avoid any displays of concern or sympathy for the youths so they will know that the counselor represents society

10.____

Questions 11-17.

DIRECTIONS: Answer Questions 11 through 17 *only* on the basis of the information and the sample report form given below.

    S. Perez and W. Carr, counselors in Dormitory C-4 at Robinson Juvenile Center, are on duty in the dormitory on September 17, 2014. At 10:15 A.M., a child suddenly begins screaming in Room 211. W. Carr runs to the room and finds a child, Bobbie Doe, lying on the floor. The child who is screaming is Bobbie Doe's roommate, Leslie Roe. Leslie says that they were both jumping on the beds and Bobbie landed wrong and fell on the floor. Bobbie is moaning now and saying, "I sure landed hard. My head hurts." The counselor sees that there is a slight amount of blood on the back of Bobbie's head, and sends Bobbie to Dr. J. Field in the medical unit to be checked for head injury and other possible injuries. As soon as Bobbie has arrived safely at the medical unit, the counselor fills out the following form.

```
┌──────────────────────────────────────────────────────────────────────┐
│                    REPORT OF ACCIDENT TO CHILD                         │
│                     (to be filled out in triplicate)                   │
│     1.   Name of injured child_____  │
│     2.   Date of injury _____  3.   Time _____   │
│     4.   Describe how injury occurred _____  │
│     5.   Signature of counselor _____  6.   Date _____   │
│   TO BE FILLED IN BY MEDICAL UNIT: _____  │
│     7.   Nature of injury 8. Treatment given _____  │
│     9.   Further treatment needed _____  │
│    10.   Signature of physician or nurse_____  11.  Date _____ │
└──────────────────────────────────────────────────────────────────────┘
```

11. How many copies of the "Report of Accident to Child" is the counselor supposed to make out?   11.____

    A. 1   B. 2   C. 3   D. 4

12. Which of the following names is the CORRECT entry for Item 1 of the report form?   12.____

    A. S. Perez   B. W. Carr   C. Leslie Roe   D. Bobbie Doe

13. Which of the following is the CORRECT entry for Item 2 of the report form?   13.____

    A. 9/17/14   B. 10/17/14   C. 10:15 A.M.   D. 10:15 P.M.

14. An accurate report of the cause of an injury is important for two purposes: First, it gives the medical unit an idea of what kinds of injuries should be looked for; second, it is a record of who or what was responsible for the accident.   14.____
Which one of the following entries for Item 4 BEST fulfills *both* of these purposes?

    A. Child complained, "My head hurts." Investigation showed some bleeding.
    B. Child was jumping on bed and fell on floor. Child reported that his head was hurt. Head was bleeding slightly.
    C. Child's roommate reported they had been jumping on beds. This behavior is dangerous and it is against the rules.
    D. Child's roommate began screaming when child was hurt. Counselor found child lying on floor and moaning.

15. Which of the following names is the CORRECT entry for Item 5 of the report form?   15.____

    A. S. Perez   B. W. Carr   C. Leslie Roe   D. J. Field

16. Which of the following is the CORRECT entry for Item 6?   16.____

    A. September, A.M., 2014   B. September 2014, 10:15 A.M.
    C. September 17, 2014   D. September 2014, Robinson

17. What information, if any, should the counselor fill in for Item 7?   17.____

    A. "Head injury"
    B. "Injuries from falling on floor"
    C. "Head injury and possible other injuries"
    D. No information

18. Many juvenile detention facilities focus on vocational training, rather than academic training, for children of high school age.
Of the following, the BEST reason for emphasizing vocational training is that

    A. most juveniles in a detention facility have a lower than average IQ and frequently are not able to do academic high school work
    B. detained juveniles of high school age usually benefit more from job training
    C. a high school diploma cannot be awarded in the state to a person under legal detention
    D. qualified teachers of academic subjects are in short supply and their higher salaries would be a drain on the detention center's budget

18._____

19. During a visiting period between parents and children in a juvenile detention center, a heated argument between a parent and his child is observed by the counselor on duty. The counselor succeeds in stopping the argument but not in solving the problem that led to the argument.
Which of the following would be the BEST action for the counselor to take next?

    A. Continue his efforts to solve the problem on the parent's next visit
    B. Report the incident and the problem to his supervisor
    C. Admonish the child after the visit and explain that arguing with parents is unacceptable behavior
    D. Advise the parent that he should refrain from further visits until he can stop verbally abusing his child

19._____

Questions 20-22.

DIRECTIONS: Answer Questions 20 through 22 on the basis of the information and the list below.

The following list gives dates on which 8 children were admitted to a juvenile detention center:

Name	Admission Date
Abner, E	November 6, 2014
Alvarez, L.	October 24, 2014
Blake, G.	October 31, 2014
Charlton, M.	November 7, 2014
Davis, A.	November 8, 2014
Green, M.	November 1, 2014
Figua, J.	October 31, 2014
Smith, O.	October 25, 2014

20. The children who have been at the center for less than one week as of November 12, 2014, are:

    A. Alvarez, L.; Blake, G.; Figua, J.
    B. Abner, E.; Charlton, M.; Davis, A.
    C. Charlton, M.; Davis, A.; Green, M.
    D. Davis, A.; Green, M.; Figua, J.

20._____

21. The children who have been at the center for at least one week but less than two weeks as of November 12, 2014, are:

   21.____

  A. Blake, G.; Green, M.; Figua, J.
  B. Charlton, M.; Davis, A.; Smith, O.
  C. Alvarez, L.; Blake, G.; Figua, J.
  D. Blake, G.; Figua, J.; Smith, O.

22. The children who have been at the center for at least two weeks but less than three weeks as of November 12, 2014, are:

   22.____

  A. Alvarez, L.; Smith, O.
  B. Alvarez, L.; Blake, G.; Green, M.; Figua, J.
  C. Charlton, M.; Davis, A.
  D. Alvarez, L.; Blake, G.; Figua, J.

23. A child in a juvenile detention center dormitory signs a sick call sheet and asks to see a doctor. The counselor on duty in the dormitory suspects that the child is not really sick but wants attention.
Which of the following would be the BEST action for the counselor to take?

   23.____

  A. Remove the child's name from the sick call sheet and arrange for the child to be a leader in the next round of group activities
  B. Remove the child's name from the sick call sheet and explain to the child that making a fuss over trivial matters is not the way to become noticed
  C. Allow the child to be examined by the doctor and make no comment to the child about the suspicion that he is not sick
  D. Allow the child to be examined by the doctor but tell the child that faking will not be tolerated in the future

24. A counselor supervising a visiting area in a detention center is also acting as a representative of the center. The visiting public's impression of the center depends partly on the counselor's behavior.
Which of the following would be the *most appropriate* behavior for a counselor supervising a visiting area?

   24.____

  A. Urge the visitors to help rehabilitate the children
  B. Advise the children to avoid visitors who seem to have problems
  C. Apologize to the visitors for the state statutes on juvenile justice
  D. Watch the visiting area carefully and treat all present politely

25. Deviants are labeled as such by those with the power and prestige to establish the rules of society as a whole; individuals who seriously defy these rules are considered deviants. However, deviants often reject society's negative labels and endeavor to use their subculture as a base to acquire power and prestige in the general society. If successful, their former deviancy may come to be regarded by society generally as a normal variation of behavior. This statement means, *most nearly,* that

   25.____

  A. power plays an important role in society's definition of deviancy
  B. power and prestige are not sought by deviants
  C. deviants who reject society's negative labels acquire power
  D. power is acquired by defying society's rules

KEY (CORRECT ANSWERS)

1.	A	11.	C
2.	C	12.	D
3.	D	13.	A
4.	D	14.	B
5.	C	15.	B
6.	A	16.	C
7.	C	17.	D
8.	C	18.	B
9.	C	19.	B
10.	B	20.	B

21.	A
22.	A
23.	C
24.	D
25.	A

TEST 3

DIRECTIONS: Each question or incomplete statement is followed by several suggested answers or completions. Select the one that BEST answers the question or completes the statement. *PRINT THE LETTER OF THE CORRECT ANSWER IN THE SPACE AT THE RIGHT.*

1. A child in a juvenile detention center tells his counselor that he is very worried about problems at home and the ability of his parents to cope with these problems. Which of the following would be the BEST action for the counselor to take?

    1.____

    A. Impress upon the child the fact that if he had not misbehaved he would be home helping his parents
    B. Report the child's concern to the center's social worker
    C. Explain to the child that excessive concern about parents and their problems may damage his normal development
    D. Instruct the child to avoid the fate of his parents through discipline and self-improvement

2. Some experts believe that much delinquency is not really deeply rooted, but is an immediate response to an immediate situation.
Which of the following is the BEST example of a solution to the type of situation described in the preceding quotation?

    2.____

    A. Improved recreation programs for youth in slums
    B. Special rehabilitative efforts for aggressive delinquents
    C. Special anti-theft devices installed on automobiles
    D. Improved school counseling programs for slow learners

Questions 3-9.

DIRECTIONS: Answer Questions 3 through 9 *only* on the basis of the information in the passage below.

Laws concerning juveniles make it clear that the function of the courts is to treat delinquents, not to punish them. Many years ago, children were detained in jails or police lockups along with adult offenders. Today, however, it is recognized that separate detention is important for the protection of the children. Detention is now regarded as part of the treatment process.

Detention is not an ordinary child care job. On the one hand, it must be distinguished from mere shelter care, which is a custodial program for children whose families cannot care for them adequately. On the other hand, it must be distinguished from treatment in mental health institutions, which is meant for children who have very serious mental or psychological problems. The children in a detention facility are there because they have run into trouble with the law, and because they must be kept in safe custody for a short period until the court decides the final action to be taken in each child's case.

The Advisory Committee on Detention and Shelter Care has outlined several basic objectives for a good detention service. One objective is secure custody. Like adults who are being detained until their cases come up before the court, children too will often want to escape from detention. Security measures must be adequate to prevent ordinary escape attempts, although at the same time a jail-like atmosphere should be avoided. Another objective is to provide constructive activities for the children and to give individual guidance through casework and group sessions. A final objective is to study each child individually so that useful information can be provided for court action and so that the mental, emotional, or other problems that have contributed to the child's difficulties can be identified.

3. According to the above passage, laws concerning juveniles make it clear that the *main* aim of the courts in handling young offenders is to   3._____

    A. punish juvenile delinquents
    B. provide treatment for juvenile delinquents
    C. relieve the families of juvenile delinquents
    D. counsel families which have juvenile delinquents

4. The passage *implies* that the former practice of locking up juveniles along with adults was   4._____

    A. *good,* because it was more efficient than providing separate facilities
    B. *good,* because children could then be protected by the adults
    C. *bad,* because the children were not safe
    D. *bad,* because delinquents need mental health treatment

5. The passage says that a detention center differs from a shelter care facility in that the children in a detention center   5._____

    A. have been placed there permanently by their families or by the courts
    B. come from families who cannot or will not care for them
    C. have serious mental or psychological problems
    D. are in trouble with the law and must be kept in safe custody temporarily

6. The passage mentions one specific way in which detained juveniles are like detained adults. This similarity is that both detained juveniles and detained adults   6._____

    A. may try to escape from the detention facility
    B. have been convicted of serious crimes
    C. usually come from bad family backgrounds
    D. have mental or emotional problems

7. The passage lists several basic objectives that were out- lined by the Advisory Committee on Detention and Child Care. Which one of the following aims is NOT given in the list of Advisory Committee objectives?   7._____

    A. Separating juvenile offenders from adult offenders
    B. Providing secure custody
    C. Giving individual guidance
    D. Providing useful information for court action

8. The passage mentions a "custodial program." This means, *most nearly,*   8._____

    A. janitor services
    B. a program to prevent jail escapes
    C. caretaking services for dependent children
    D. welfare payments to families with children

9. The passage says that "security measures" are needed in a detention center PRIMARILY in order to
   9.____

   A. prevent unauthorized persons from entering
   B. prevent juveniles from escaping
   C. ensure that records are safeguarded for court action
   D. create a jail-like atmosphere

10. Juveniles at a detention center are permitted to smoke cigarettes during smoking periods if they are over fourteen and have the written consent of their parents. A juvenile over fourteen, but without parental written consent, repeatedly asks a counselor for a cigarette during a smoking period.
    10.____
    Which of the following would be the BEST action for the counselor to take?

    A. Tell the juvenile to get a cigarette from another child but to make sure that the counselor does not see him smoking
    B. Give the juvenile a cigarette if, in the counselor's opinion, it would help the juvenile's adjustment to the center
    C. Explain to the juvenile that he will be permitted to smoke when he secures his parents' consent
    D. Urge the juvenile to display maturity and not bother the counselor with trivial requests

11. Children newly admitted to a juvenile detention center are first assigned to the reception center dormitory where a daytime counselor explains the rules and regulations of the center.
    11.____
    Which of the following would be the BEST way for the counselor to insure that the children understand these rules? Explain

    A. *thoroughly* but do not allow questions by the children, because too many questions would tend to confuse them
    B. *briefly,* but give a short written quiz to the children right afterward, giving a more thorough explanation to those who fail
    C. *thoroughly* and advise the children to save any questions for practical situations as they arise during their stay at the detention center
    D. *thoroughly* and allow a question and answer period at the end

12. A counselor in a detention center confiscates the contraband he has found in a child's possession.
    12.____
    Which of the following is the BEST action for the counselor to take *next?*

    A. Report the incident to his superior
    B. Inform the child that serious consequences will follow any future incidents of this nature
    C. Turn the contraband over to the nearest police precinct
    D. Arrange for the contraband's burning at the borough sanitation incinerator

13. The family is a vital component in any program of juvenile delinquency prevention and treatment.
    13.____
    Which of the following would probably contribute LEAST to making families function better?

    A.   Better housing for the family
    B.   More restrictive legislation regarding divorce and adultery
    C.   Increased employment opportunities for members of the family
    D.   Expanded family planning education

14. When a social worker tells the counselor that a child is "culturally deprived," the counse-   14._____
lor is *most likely* to find that the child

    A.   is illegitimate
    B.   comes from a broken home
    C.   is a "slow learner" and might be slightly retarded
    D.   has not had as much opportunity or motivation as most children to develop academic skills

15. Recreational programs are important in the success of a rehabilitation program.   15._____
Of the following, the BEST method for the counselor to use to insure that the time allotted for recreation achieves the greatest possible success in rehabilitation would be to

    A.   specialize in one or two competitive sports so that a youth will have sufficient practice to win and experience the accomplishment of victory over his peers
    B.   keep the recreation time quiet, because, if adolescents get excited and worked up during a play session, they will be behavior problems for the rest of the day
    C.   include non-competitive activities in addition to the usual athletic competition since many of the detained youths have never successfully competed anywhere
    D.   make it clear that recreation time is a reward for good behavior and can be withheld as a punishment

16. Many family research experts believe that the relationship between parent and child in   16._____
this country has a great influence on the personality and development of the child. Which of the following statements BEST represents the opinion of most of these experts concerning parental influence in the child's personality development?

    A.   Mothers and fathers have approximately equal impact on their children, regardless of the age or sex of the child.
    B.   Fathers have very little impact on their children until the child is 16, after which they have approximately equal impact with the mother.
    C.   Mothers and fathers tend to have different effects on their children, depending partly on the age and sex of both parent and child.
    D.   The mother's influence on the child, regardless of the sex of the child, is overwhelming up to the age of six, after which the father's influence is predominant, regardless of the sex of the child.

17. A growing child needs group activity in order to develop socially. A gang is one example   17._____
of such a group. Joining a gang often answers a boy's needs for companionship and adventure. He gets the feeling of belonging and of loyalty to the group. If the gang is delinquent, the tougher the boy is, the more recognition he gets from the gang. He may also find the discipline he needs because gangs frequently develop their own codes and rules of behavior and demand that their members rigidly abide by them.
On the basis of the foregoing statement, if a child joins a gang, which of the following is *most probably* TRUE?

    A.   He will become an adult criminal.
    B.   He could not find enough companionship and sense of belonging outside the gang.

C. The gang was formed to commit acts of violence.
D. He has been in a detention facility several times already.

18. There are many theories of the causes of delinquent behavior. One approach sees delin-   18.____
quent behavior as the normal response of many adolescents to conditions of social and
economic deprivation characteristic of the lower class. This statement *implies* that

A. delinquent behavior is a neurotic response to repeated personal failure
B. the root of the delinquency problem is to be found in destructive family relationships
C. delinquency is more related to a particular kind of social environment than it is to
individual character
D. delinquent behavior can be treated by modifying individual patterns of personal
feeling,behavior, and relationships

———

KEYS (CORRECT ANSWERS)

1.	B	11.	D
2.	C	12.	A
3.	B	13.	B
4.	C	14.	D
5.	D	15.	C
6.	A	16.	C
7.	A	17.	B
8.	C	18.	C
9.	B		
10.	C		

———

EXAMINATION SECTION
TEST 1

DIRECTIONS: Each question or incomplete statement is followed by several suggested answers or completions. Select the one that BEST answers the question or completes the statement. *PRINT THE LETTER OF THE CORRECT ANSWER IN THE SPACE AT THE RIGHT.*

1. A youth worker asks his supervisor what to do about his gang group whose members have informed him that they are planning to *go down* on another group for *jumping* one of their members on his way home from school.
   It would be best for the supervisor to recommend that the worker should FIRST

   A. individually question the members of his group about the incident
   B. engage the group members in activities outside of the neighborhood
   C. arrange a mediation meeting involving both groups
   D. report the information to police to avoid further trouble

   1._____

2. A youth worker tells his supervisor that the owner of a local bowling alley has asked him to bring his gang group over for recreation. A financial arrangement beneficial to the worker was suggested as part of the plan.
   The supervisor should advise the worker to

   A. refuse the offer because he should avoid entanglements that might compromise the agency or his professional conduct
   B. refuse the offer because he should avoid contact with the business community
   C. accept the offer but refuse payment because he should utilize all resources offered to gang members
   D. accept the offer but refuse payment because he can use the situation to establish a relationship with a member of the business community

   2._____

3. Assume that a youth worker who previously had important responsibilities complains to his supervisor about having to share periodic office coverage. This employee has been back for a few months after a serious illness and is not yet able to resume all of his previous responsibilities, but is well enough to function as a worker.
   The BEST way for the supervisor to handle this complaint is to

   A. refer the problem to his area administrator because of the special nature of the case
   B. excuse the employee from office coverage
   C. suggest to the employee that he may be well enough to take on his previous responsibilities again
   D. tell the employee that office coverage must be shared by all workers in the unit

   3._____

4. During a unit staff meeting, several youth workers raise objections to a certain youth services agency policy and make suggestions for revision of the policy that seem to the supervisor to have considerable merit.
   The MOST appropriate action for the supervisor to take would be to

   4._____

A. allow the workers to interpret the policy according to their suggestions, which relate to the needs of this neighborhood
B. inform the workers that policy changes must be initiated and implemented by higher administrative personnel of the agency
C. help the workers prepare a proposal outlining their suggestions to be submitted by the unit to higher administrative personnel
D. report to his administrator that his workers object to the policy and that considerable revision is required

5. Which of the following methods available to the supervisor of youth workers is usually MOST effective in facilitating communication with his subordinates?   5._____

    A. Weekly staff meetings   B. Memoranda
    C. Unscheduled conferences   D. Work shops

6. Several youths who belong to a gang group come to the supervisor with a problem that should have been handled by their assigned youth worker. As they talk to the supervisor, the youths also make strong complaints about their worker.   6._____
Of the following, it would be advisable for the supervisor to

    A. ignore the complaints at this time because it is risky to accept reports from gang members without further investigation
    B. report the incident to the area administrator and ask him to deal administratively with this worker
    C. review the worker's records and discuss the problem with him and the youths before taking further action
    D. have the worker transferred to another unit because he seems to be in danger of attack by these youths

7. Of the following, the factor that the supervisor should consider MOST important in evaluating a youth worker's performance is   7._____

    A. how frequently he asks for guidance
    B. his willingness to be helpful and cooperative
    C. his consistency in keeping his recording up to date
    D. his interest in his group members and his effectiveness in dealing with them

8. Assume that a citizens' group addresses a letter of commendation to a supervisor praising the youth workers on his staff for their extraordinary service in helping to deal with several emergencies involving youth in the area.   8._____
Of the following, it would be advisable for the supervisor to FIRST

    A. send the letter to the director of field operations
    B. call in the staff member who was most helpful and commend him in private
    C. write a letter of thanks to the citizens' group in the name of his staff
    D. share this commendation with his staff and his area administrator

9. A worker reports to his supervisor that one of his group members has begun to experiment with marijuana. The worker feels uneasy about handling the situation and asks for guidance.
    The supervisor should advise the worker to

    A. ignore the situation since most youths experiment with marijuana
    B. refer the youth to a drug prevention program
    C. confront the youth and discuss the situation with him
    D. discuss the situation with the youth's parents

10. In a supervisory conference, a worker asks for guidance about how to handle the problem of a 22-year-old dropout who wants to return to school in the daytime to obtain a high school diploma so that he can apply to a community college. The worker has contacted the youth's former school, but the principal refuses to take the youth back because of his age.
    Of the following, the supervisor's BEST approach would be to advise the worker to

    A. contact the district school superintendent's office and request an exception in the case of this youth
    B. tell the youth's parents to submit an appeal to the Board of Education
    C. refer the youth to a vocational training program instead
    D. urge the youth to attend evening high school and work during the day

10

11. A youth worker tells his superior he has definite evidence that one of his group members is *dealing*, but hesitates to identify the youth because he does not want to violate the principle of confidentiality.
    The supervisor should

    A. give the worker a direct order to identify the youth and take disciplinary action if the worker refuses
    B. reassign this worker to another group since he seems to be over-identifying with this youth
    C. discuss with the worker the reasons for reporting illegal acts and clarify agency policy and the need to enforce it
    D. visit and observe the group himself in order to identify the youth who is *dealing*

11

12. During his review of workers' recordings, a supervisor finds that one of his workers refers most youths who ask him about employment to a job placement agency after interviewing them only once.
    Of the following, the BEST advice the supervisor can give this worker is:

    A. Workers should try to find suitable openings in the neighborhood before referring youths to a job placement agency
    B. As a rule, a worker should interview youths seeking employment more than once in order to determine their needs and prepare them before referring them to an outside agency
    C. The youths are probably asking the worker to help them find employment in order to get attention and emotional support and are not really ready to get jobs
    D. Workers should make every effort to convince youths to go back to school and refer them for jobs only as a last resort

13. In a discussion with her supervisor about one of her group members, a female youth worker reports that she is planning to encourage 18-year-old Maria, who was born in Puerto Rico and is employed, to leave home because her father is very domineering. It would be appropriate for the supervisor to

    A.   support the worker because an 18-year-old girl who has a job needs to be more independent
    B.   advise the worker not to encourage Maria to leave home at this time and refer Maria's father to a casework agency
    C.   advise the worker not to encourage Maria to leave home and try to help Maria's mother to assert a more active role
    D.   determine whether the worker realizes that Maria's father may be assuming the patriarchal role which would be traditional for him

14. A youth worker tells his supervisor that he feels that he does not have enough leeway in serving his group and must rigidly follow too many regulations and procedures. Of the following, the BEST way for the supervisor to help this worker is to

    A.   tell him that as long as he uses good judgment he need not worry about regulations and procedures
    B.   compliment the worker whenever he interprets regulations and procedures less rigidly
    C.   ask him for program suggestions and assure him that his ideas will be considered
    D.   give him additional authority and responsibility

15. A supervisor learns that a youth worker with considerable experience has recently been acting hostile to his group and has not been providing services requested by the members.
The supervisor's FIRST action should be to discuss this behavior with the worker and

    A.   suggest that he consult with a therapist about his unconscious motives
    B.   try to help him understand why he is acting hostile
    C.   suggest to him that he may not like the group
    D.   point out that the group may not react to the worker's hostility

16. A youth worker asks his supervisor for guidance about a 15-year-old youth who had been one of the most constructive members of his group, but has recently been getting into trouble. The youth's father died ten years ago, and his mother has just remarried. The supervisor should help the worker to realize that the youth

    A.   is probably going through a crisis and should be given special attention
    B.   probably dislikes his stepfather and is misbehaving in the hope of being placed away from home
    C.   will stop misbehaving if his present conduct is not taken too seriously
    D.   should be warned that further misbehavior must be reported to his stepfather

17. During a weekly conference with his supervisor, a worker reports that a youth in his group has told him that his father is *messing around* with his 13-year-old sister. When the sister confided in the youth, she said that the father threatened to kill her if she told anyone that he was having sex with her, and the youth is frightened.
The supervisor should FIRST

    A. call the father into his office on the pretext of discussing the youth's problems in order to assess the situation
    B. have the worker report the situation to the local juvenile aid police officer
    C. have the worker report the situation immediately to the local child protective services unit of the Bureau of Child Welfare
    D. call the sister into the office in order to obtain the facts for himself

17.____

18. A youth worker who has a friend in central office is continually spreading rumors that he claims to have heard from his *connections downtown.* These rumors often sound true and are upsetting to staff.
The MOST advisable action for the supervisor of this unit to take at this point would be to

    A. tell his staff to disregard the stories spread by this worker
    B. report the worker to the director of field operations and request that he be reprimanded for his behavior
    C. arrange the worker's assignments so that he will have nothing more to do with central office
    D. tell the worker privately that his rumors are creating a morale problem and he must stop spreading them at once

18.____

19. A supervisor of a youth services unit has interviewed the father of an 18-year-old youth who says that the boy has been stealing, moody, and *hangs around with a bunch of no-good junkies.* The supervisor has reason to believe that the boy is experimenting with hard drugs, but the father does not seem to be able to cope with this because of his fears and his pride in the family.
When the supervisor assigns a worker to this case, it would be appropriate for him to tell the worker to start out by

    A. telling the father that the boy is on hard drugs and should be in treatment
    B. suggesting to the father to have the boy put under observation by the youth division of the police department
    C. talking with the father about widespread drug use and narcotic addiction among middle-class youth in order to relieve him of his guilt
    D. assuring the father that confidentiality will be upheld and that he should feel free to discuss his fears

19.____

20. A supervisor finds it necessary to intervene in a heated argument between two of his workers. One worker, who comes from a middle class background, insists that drug abuse is due mainly to psychological problems, while the other worker, who was brought up in the ghetto, insists that drug abuse is due to the pressures of *the street*.
The BEST way for the supervisor to handle this dispute would be to

    A. assign the middle-class worker to the office since he is probably having difficulty working in the street
    B. tell the workers to *cool it* and separate them in their assignments in the field
    C. help the workers to see that both are partly right and could probably learn from each other if they could manage to have a calm discussion
    D. give both workers reliable literature on drug abuse so that they will get the facts in proper perspective

Questions 21-30.

DIRECTIONS: In Questions 21 through 30, choose the lettered word or expression which is CLOSEST to the meaning of the first word or expression, *as used most frequently by street-oriented youths and members of youth gangs*. Do not try to give the usually accepted or dictionary definition of the word or expression.

21. *dyke*

    A. *crack* package
    C. opium addict
    B. packet of narcotics
    D. female homosexual

22. *burned out*

    A. kicked the habit
    C. pulled a robbery
    B. took an overdose
    D. challenged a rival gang

23. *drop acid*

    A. buy LSD
    C. stay off LSD
    B. take LSD
    D. sell LSD

24. *juicehead*

    A. homosexual
    C. *ice* user
    B. natural food faddist
    D. alcoholic

25. *threads*

    A. popped veins
    C. complications
    B. police connections
    D. clothes

26. *out of sight*

    A. conventional
    C. informed
    B. superb
    D. forbidden

27. *hairy*

    A. difficult
    C. torn into shreds
    B. smart
    D. mentally disturbed

28. *blowing snow*

    A. cheating   B. giving up
    C. sniffing cocaine   D. keeping secret

28.____

29. *feed your head*

    A. steal food   B. fall asleep
    C. act crazy   D. take drugs

29.____

30. *racked up*

    A. taken an overdose   B. drunk
    C. upset   D. hiding from the police

30.____

KEY (CORRECT ANSWERS)

1.	A	11.	C	21.	D
2.	A	12.	B	22.	A
3.	D	13.	D	23.	B
4.	C	14.	C	24.	D
5.	A	15.	B	25.	D
6.	C	16.	A	26.	B
7.	D	17.	C	27.	A
8.	D	18.	D	28.	C
9.	C	19.	D	29.	D
10.	D	20.	C	30.	C

TEST 2

DIRECTIONS: Each question or incomplete statement is followed by several suggested answers or completions. Select the one that BEST answers the question or completes the statement. *PRINT THE LETTER OF THE CORRECT ANSWER IN THE SPACE AT THE RIGHT.*

1. A youth comes running into the unit office and reports that a Black youth has been killed in a fight between Black and Asian gang members and that Black adults in the community are in an uproar and are threatening violence against Asians.
Of the following, the supervisor should FIRST

    A. call Black and Asian adult community leaders into his office in order to enlist their help in preventing further violence
    B. assign as many Black and Asian workers as possible to the respective gang groups in an attempt to *cool it*
    C. get immediate field reports from workers in the affected areas in order to get an accurate picture of the situation
    D. call Black and Asian gang leaders into his office for a mediation meeting

1.____

2. The *Social Seven,* a gang group, have not had a gang fight for the past 16 months, and most of the members have not been involved in any other anti-social incidents recently. The assigned worker suggests termination of services to this group and asks his supervisor to be reassigned to the *Spanish Lads,* a real *down* group.
The appropriate action for the supervisor to take at this point would be to

    A. reassign the worker since the *Social Seven* are not likely to get into trouble at this stage
    B. keep the worker with the *Social Seven* since a gang group's behavior is unpredictable
    C. set up meetings with the worker to discuss the pros and cons of termination of services to the *Social Seven*
    D. advise the worker to continue working with the *Social Seven* but to make less contact with them and drift away gradually

2.____

3. A 15-year-old youth who attends high school comes into the office at a time when he should be on his way to school and asks for help in finding a part-time job after school.
The BEST way for the worker to handle this situation is to

    A. interview the youth about a job so that he does not waste the day
    B. refuse to interview the youth at the time and advise him to go to school and return at the end of the day
    C. interview the youth and determine his reasons for wanting a job
    D. phone the youth's parents and advise them that the youth is out of school that day

3.____

4. A worker has had considerable discussion with a youth about his problems and decides   4.____
that he should be referred to another agency for special treatment.
Which of the following would be the MOST appropriate way for the worker to handle
the referral?

   A. Send the youth to the agency with a brief note since the youth can best explain his
problems.
   B. Phone the intake worker of the agency to discuss the youth's case and have the
agency make the initial contact with the youth.
   C. Talk to the youth about the referral process before and after making contact and
discussing the youth's case with a representative of the agency.
   D. Offer the youth a choice of several suitable agencies and have him make the initial
contact.

5. After preparing a youth for referral to a treatment center, a youth worker should usually   5.____
maintain close contact with both the youth and his therapist.
This continued contact is important MAINLY because the

   A. worker will be able to take the supportive role needed to keep the youth in treat-
ment
   B. youth will be able to get a more realistic picture of the treatment process
   C. worker will have a chance to get first-hand knowledge about the treatment process
   D. therapist will have a chance to meet the worker

6. In order to make suitable referrals and use community agencies to the greatest extent   6.____
possible, it is MOST important for the youth worker to know

   A. what services the agencies have to offer
   B. the locations of the central offices of the agencies
   C. how the agencies are funded
   D. prominent staff members of the agencies

7. A supervisor who has been working with his staff to implement a job program for youths   7.____
in his area drafts a program proposal to submit to the director of field operations. The
items covered in the proposal are resources, population to be served, priorities, role of
the agency, participation of the community in the program, staff needs, and budget
needs.
Of the following, a KEY factor which has been OMITTED is

   A. names of interested community leaders
   B. documentation of need for the program
   C. approval of the unit staff
   D. approval of the community

8. A worker comes to his supervisor for help in handling the problem of a 14-year-old youth who is talking about *splitting* from home. The worker has developed a close relationship with this youth and his family and does not consider the situation to be serious enough to justify the youth's desire to leave home.
It would be advisable for the supervisor to

    A.   help the worker to see that he is over-identifying with the youth and his family and should become less involved
    B.   have the worker contact the youth division in the local precinct because experience indicates that this youth will probably run away from home
    C.   discuss with the worker some specific ways to help this youth by *talking it out* with him and his parents
    D.   help the worker to see that this is a big *put on* by the youth to get attention

8.____

9. An inexperienced female youth worker in a supervisor's unit has been working with a group of 13- to 15-year-old girls. The worker's records indicate that whenever the girls start talking about sex, having babies, and abortions, the worker becomes very formal and does her best to get them to change the subject.
The supervisor should

    A.   encourage the worker to continue to act as an authority figure with the girls and to avoid talking about sex with them
    B.   realize that the worker has a hang-up about sex and is unlikely to be able to handle girls with precocious sexual knowledge and behavior
    C.   tell the worker that she is being too hard on these girls and will have a better relationship with them if she can talk about sex on their level
    D.   realize that the girls may be *testing* the worker and that she may not be confident enough to handle this yet and needs the supervisor's help and support

9.____

10. A youth worker in a supervisor's unit is unusually outspoken and assertive and often gets into heated discussions with colleagues in the unit and youth workers from other agencies over services the worker feels are needed by his group.
The BEST way for the supervisor to attempt to resolve this problem is to

    A.   help the other workers in the unit to stay *cool* when this worker gets excited about his group's unmet needs
    B.   have the worker transferred to another unit
    C.   help the worker to become more diplomatic with colleagues and representatives of outside agencies
    D.   encourage the worker to keep being assertive because it is the only way to get results

10.____

11. A recently arrived Hispanic youth who speaks no English comes to a youth services agency office asking for help in finding employment.
The supervisor's FIRST step should be to

    A.   refer the youth to an employment agency where Spanish is spoken
    B.   refer the youth to a program for learning English as a second language
    C.   assign a Spanish-speaking worker to interview the youth and evaluate his needs
    D.   assign the youth to a worker and suggest that a job be developed for the youth where English will not be needed

11.____

12. As a result of several meetings held with neighborhood residents by a youth worker, the community is becoming more interested in problems of local youths. After several months, the community group makes a request through the worker for help from the youth services agency in establishing a small, locally-run youth center.
It would be BEST for the youth worker's supervisor to

    12.____

    A. suggest to the worker that the program plan may be premature
    B. tell the worker to advise the community group to raise funds for the center in the neighborhood
    C. have the worker help the group to prepare their program request for submission to higher levels in the agency
    D. submit the community's plan to the program planning committee

13. Of the following, the CHIEF cause of death among people between 15-25 years of age is

    13.____

    A. lead poisoning
    B. drug abuse
    C. suicide
    D. malnutrition

14. Some psychiatrists and psychologists have a low opinion of the street club worker's function and his value in changing the behavior of anti-social youths.
Of the following, the MOST serious consequence of such an attitude is that it may

    14.____

    A. cause street club workers to resent other professionals
    B. discourage street club workers from referring youths to psychologists and psychiatrists
    C. result in transference of this negative attitude about street club workers to their group members
    D. make it difficult for street club workers to obtain professional training

15. Assume that the unit supervisor observes that a youth who is waiting in the office for his first interview with a worker is nervous, sweating, yawning, and constantly blowing his nose.
It would be important for the supervisor to

    15.____

    A. discuss his observations and possible reasons for the youth's behavior with the worker who interviews him
    B. call the youth into his office for a brief talk in order to observe him more closely
    C. greet the youth casually and try to put him at ease before the interview
    D. discuss the youth's behavior with him at length before he is interviewed by the worker

16. Assume that a group of mothers comes to the local youth services agency office with the complaint that their pre-adolescent children are in danger of getting into trouble because there are very few recreational facilities available for them in the neighborhood. They ask the supervisor for his help in developing more recreational resources.
Of the following, the MOST appropriate action for the supervisor to take FIRST would be to

    16.____

    A. refer the matter to the department of recreation
    B. discuss the request with administrative officials of the youth services agency
    C. discuss the situation with workers assigned in the neighborhood since they should have pertinent information about recreational facilities
    D. invite mothers to a meeting with other interested community people in an effort to properly identify the problem

17. The president of the neighborhood block association invites the supervisor of the local   17.____
youth services agency unit for the first time to a meeting called to discuss community
problems caused by the anti-social behavior of gang youth in the area.
The supervisor should welcome the opportunity to attend this meeting MAINLY
because it would enable him to

    A. gain some insight into the feelings of neighborhood adults about gang youths and
explain to them how agency workers relate to anti-social youths
    B. gain additional insight into the gang members' feelings and concerns about neigh-
borhood adults
    C. assure members of the block association that the youth services agency is making
substantial progress in curbing anti-social behavior of local youth
    D. gather specific complaints from neighborhood adults about the behavior of individ-
ual youths so that he can assign workers to give additional attention to curbing
their anti-social acts

18. Assume that a youth worker newly assigned to a gang group becomes friendly with Dano   18.____
a member of the group, and wants Dano to help him make his first contacts with the other
members.
Before proceeding further, it is important for the worker to

    A. inform Dano that he has been assigned to the area by the youth services agency to
work with the group
    B. question Dano about the group without identifying himself as a representative of
the youth services agency
    C. talk about sports and other matters that would interest Dano and give no indication
that he is a youth worker assigned to the group
    D. ask Dano to arrange for the worker to meet with the group as a whole

19. Assume that a youth worker recently assigned to a gang group has been able to make   19.____
friends with a few of the members individually. However, the more powerful members of
the group seem to resent his presence in the area.
At this point, the worker should

    A. continue to relate to the individual members of the group
    B. try to convince the leader of the group that he can do a lot for them
    C. leave the area because he may be in danger of physical attack by the hostile mem-
bers
    D. invite the entire group to go out with him for refreshments

20. A youth worker reports to his assigned area and is told by one of his gang group mem-   20.____
bers that the group is angry with him and wants him to leave the neighborhood.
The worker can BEST approach this situation by

    A. locating the other members and trying to find out what their attitude is toward him
    B. leaving the neighborhood for the day in the hope that the situation will resolve itself
    C. asking his supervisor for temporary reassignment to another group until the hostile
members *cool off*
    D. arranging an informal gathering with refreshments and inviting the hostile mem-
bers

21. Several workers present their supervisor with excellent proposals for programs with their assigned groups. However, the supervisor finds that staff and budget resources are far from adequate to implement these programs as planned by the workers.
Of the following, it would usually be advisable for the supervisor to

    21._____

    A. request additional funds to carry out the programs
    B. ask the workers to review the programs and resubmit them after making revisions wherever possible to reduce staff and funding requirements
    C. approve the programs on a priority basis, implementing first those planned for the groups with the most serious problems
    D. ask his administrator for guidance on how to allocate staff and funds

22. A supervisor has been directed by his area administrator to assign one of his workers to a special task to be completed within a month and gives the assignment to a worker whom he considers most capable of doing the job. The worker seems hesitant but accepts the assignment without comment, even though he is told that he will be relieved of some of his regular work. However, when the supervisor checks on the worker's progress a week later, he finds that he has not started to work on the assignment.
The BEST action for the supervisor to take is to

    22._____

    A. give part of the assignment to another worker since it must be completed to meet the deadline
    B. report the worker to the area administrator for insubordination
    C. remind the worker about the assignment and assure him of your confidence that he will complete it on time
    D. reassign the entire task to another worker

23. Assume that the supervisor of a youth services agency unit makes demands upon a new worker which are beyond the worker's present capabilities.
Of the following, the MOST probable result of the supervisor's actions would be to

    23._____

    A. give the worker an incentive to learn at a faster pace
    B. undermine the worker's confidence and inhibit him from fulfilling his present capabilities
    C. demonstrate the need for formal in-service training before a new worker is assigned to a unit
    D. encourage the worker to seek professional training in order to improve his performance

24. A worker reports to his supervisor that one of the subgroups in a youth council is led by a youth who has many constructive ideas but whose contribution is limited because of his rivalry with the elected president of the council.
Of the following, the supervisor should advise the worker to

    24._____

    A. allow the youths to settle this problem without outside assistance
    B. tell the leader of the sub-group to withhold his ideas until he becomes an elected officer
    C. attempt to curb the rivalry so that the leader of the sub-group can get his ideas across
    D. appoint the leader of the sub-group to the executive board of the council

25. A worker tells his supervisor that he is troubled because the youths in his group are con-   25._____
tinually asking him personal questions, and he does not know how to answer them.
Of the following, it would be BEST for the supervisor to advise the worker to

    A. try to find out why the youths are asking these questions
    B. point out to the youths that it would not be professional to answer personal ques-
tions
    C. try to give a brief, truthful answer and immediately redirect the youths to their own
problems
    D. tell the youths everything they want to know in order to foster a friendly relationship

26. The supervisor should advise new staff members that, in working with adolescent   26._____
groups, it is important for the worker to give guidance

    A. at every opportunity
    B. only when the members ask for it
    C. without becoming the group leader himself
    D. to a greater extent to the less aggressive members

27. A youth worker reports to his supervisor that the behavior of the youths in his group is   27._____
fairly orderly while he is with them, but that roughhousing breaks out as soon as he
leaves them.
Of the following, the MOST reasonable explanation for this change in their behavior is
that

    A. the worker is not exercising enough control
    B. this is the typical behavior pattern of anti-social youth
    C. the worker is probably too strict and *tight* with them
    D. the youths dislike the worker and resent his presence

28. Most adolescents hesitate to risk disapproval by showing their fears and anxieties. How-   28._____
ever, repressing these fears and anxieties may lead to more serious psychological problems.
The one of the following which would be the MOST appropriate method for a youth
worker to use in order to help his group overcome their fears and anxieties would be to
schedule

    A. regular sessions during which the members are encouraged to discuss their fears
and anxieties
    B. activities that are not likely to produce fears and anxieties
    C. programs that give special emphasis to wrestling, boxing, and competitive sports
    D. talks by professionals on typical adolescent fears and anxieties

29. In attempting to achieve constructive goals by means of programs, it is particularly impor-   29._____
tant for the youth worker to be aware that delinquent youths

    A. are usually more interested in activities that take them away from their immediate
neighborhood
    B. tend to *act out* feelings and express themselves by means of activity rather than
verbal exchange
    C. tend to participate more actively if the youth worker takes a passive role while the
program is in progress
    D. are best suited to activities that require considerable sharing and integration of
effort

30. According to observers of present-day gang groups, the gang leaders often choose a member who is a minor to commit a crime for the group as a whole.
The MOST plausible reason why the gang would make such a choice is that a minor is

    30.____

    A. usually stereotyped by the police
    B. less likely to receive a long prison sentence
    C. more likely to be released on his own recognizance
    D. easier to hide from the police

KEY (CORRECT ANSWERS)

1.	C	11.	C	21.	B
2.	C	12.	C	22.	C
3.	B	13.	B	23.	B
4.	C	14.	B	24.	C
5.	A	15.	A	25.	C
6.	A	16.	D	26.	C
7.	B	17.	A	27.	C
8.	C	18.	A	28.	A
9.	D	19.	A	29.	B
10.	C	20.	A	30.	B

EXAMINATION SECTION
TEST 1

DIRECTIONS: Each question or incomplete statement is followed by several suggested answers or completions. Select the one that BEST answers the question or completes the statement. *PRINT THE LETTER OF THE CORRECT ANSWER IN THE SPACE AT THE RIGHT.*

1. In working with adolescent groups, an important point to remember is to give 1.____

    A. guidance without taking matters out of the group's hands
    B. guidance to the youth leaders only
    C. assistance only when the groups ask for it
    D. direct assistance at every opportunity

2. The BASIC purpose to be kept in mind when programming group activities for delinquent adolescents is that 2.____

    A. group activities are natural for delinquents
    B. the activities should focus on control and discipline
    C. the youths should share in the program expenses
    D. the activities should focus on total freedom of expression

3. Workers assigned to your unit are experiencing difficulties with programming group activities. The programs seen to be out of context with the problems of the youths, and the youths are reported to be bored, evasive, and non-participating.
An important factor in programming that you, as unit supervisor, must teach them is 3.____

    A. to involve the group members in the planning and implementation of all programs
    B. to include current procedures like enounter, reality therapy, and crisis intervention
    C. that they must have individual meetings with key members to enlist their aid and assistance
    D. that they are not providing enough direction and control to the group meetings

4. The one of the following groups of characteristics which MOST correctly describes anti-social adolescent groups is 4.____

    A. fraternity, mutual respect, and interest in each other
    B. group loyalty, need to retaliate, and the necessity to fight
    C. divisiveness, mistrust, and self-centeredness
    D. none of the above

5. You are supervising a new worker who tells you, during his supervisory conference, that he feels that he has not been able to help his group to re-direct their energies into productive channels.
It would be BEST for you to advise this worker that 5.____

    A. he should not be discouraged because adolescents have boundless energy that is difficult to control
    B. adolescent groups respond to planning and direction, and that he should set up some simple form of organization
    C. the conflict and competition concept of group behavior requires group psychotherapy
    D. his anxieties are getting in the way of effective work with his group

6. A new worker in the unit under your supervision shows in his recording that he has been 6.____
able to overcome his feelings of insecurity in his new role of working with his group and
to work through the initial testing period imposed on him by the group. However, during
his supervisory conference, you discover that he is extremely anxious because the group
does not seem to be verbalizing their problems with him.
You should advise this worker in conference that

    A. these are hard-core youths who do not talk about their problems
    B. his recording is weak, and should be done in process style for the next six months
    C. his anxiety is probably being communicated to the group, inhibiting them from ver-
       balizing their problems
    D. a marathon encounter with the group may help them to verbalize their problems

7. In preparation for a staff conference covering principles of working with alienated youth 7.____
groups, you assign different aspects of the subject to different workers. In his notes, the
worker who is to discuss *process in working with groups* lists the following:
    1. sensitivity to the pace of group movement
    2. resistance and resentment arising from domination by the worker
    3. time and place of meetings
An IMPORTANT part that was omitted by the worker is

    A. realistic programming
    B. awareness of *where the group is at*
    C. the importance of sensitivity training
    D. supervision

8. A youth worker reports to you in a supervisory conference that the youths in his group 8.____
are unfriendly and bossy with each other, but that when he leaves them, roughhousing
breaks out.
The MOST likely explanation for this is that

    A. he is not exercising enough control
    B. he is probably too strict and tight with them
    C. this particular group of kids usually acts this way
    D. this is unusual behavior of alienated youth

9. The SIGNIFICANT factors that would distinguish a constructive and orderly group of 9.____
adolescents from an anti-social gang are the

    A. aims, quality of the relationships, and behavior of the individuals
    B. aims, personality of the members, and locale
    C. age, problems, and behavior of the members
    D. locale, personality of the members, and leadership

10. Youth workers involved with groups of adolescent girls may have to deal with problems of 10.____
sexual acting-out. Programming for girls involved in sexual acting-out should have as its
BASIC purpose

    A. security building and developing a feeling of being needed and wanted
    B. sex information and a discussion of birth control and abortion
    C. rap sessions on dating, making out, and male-female psychology
    D. parties, dances, outings, and bus rides

11. Adolescents have many fears that they are ashamed to show because they are afraid of disapproval. Restraining these fears may lead to anxieties that could be even more troublesome.
    To help youths resolve such problems, youth service units should emphasize in their programming

    A. activities that help youths gain self-confidence
    B. rap sessions on anxiety
    C. activities that are not likely to produce fear
    D. hiking, swimming, wrestling, and basketball

    11.____

12. All of the following are purposes of group counseling EXCEPT

    A. avoidance of treating pathology as such
    B. helping clients attain a better level of functioning
    C. modifying social and familial problems
    D. resolving intra-psychic conflicts

    12.____

13. A MAJOR advantage of having group programs for local teenagers in Youth Services Agency neighborhood offices is that

    A. these programs are less expensive to operate
    B. the participating groups are mutual groups in their own environment
    C. this activity is necessary for suppressing riots
    D. such programs serve as good public relations

    13.____

14. A worker reports about his youth council that one of the sub-groups in the council revolves around a boy who has many constructive ideas. However, this boy's participation is limited due to the rivalry between him and the elected president.
    The supervisor should advise the worker to

    A. have the leader of the sub-group excluded from the council
    B. help the leader of the sub-group participate more actively
    C. tell the leader of the sub-group to *play ball* with the rest of the council
    D. let the council settle this problem without outside assistance

    14.____

15. One of your youth workers is having difficulty forming a group in a particular neighborhood. Parents in that area are upset about the idea of teenage groups. This worker plans to meet with some of these parents, and he asks your help in reaching a goal with them. As supervisor, you should advise him to approach this problem by

    A. helping the parents to see that group activities are a sign of a youth's growth, not of a lack of gratitude or affection for his parents
    B. informing the parents that it is the professional opinion of the Youth Services Agency that groups are necessary in order to serve youth constructively
    C. postponing this meeting until you can convince individual parents of the value of groups
    D. helping the parents to see that many of their teenagers are having difficulties at home and in school because they do not participate in group activities

    15.____

16. Experts have described festivals, fairs, holidays, etc. as *nothing less nor more than*   16.____
excesses provided by law and which owe their cheerful character to the release which
they bring.
The significance of this in programming unit projects is to

    A. have the workers assist the community in sponsoring fairs, block dances, etc.
    B. leave the sponsoring of fairs, dances, etc. to associations affiliated with the police
       department
    C. avoid involving large groups of people in public affairs because of the danger of
       fights, riots, etc.
    D. use a good part of the unit's budget for fairs, dances, bazaars, etc.

17. Which one of the groups listed below has the following four characteristics: 17.____
    1. Basic depressive character
    2. Intolerance for frustration and pain
    3. Lack of meaningful objects
    4. Artificial technique to maintain self-regard?

    A. College students   B. Drug abusers
    C. Adolescents   D. Alienated youth

18. The MOST important consideration in evaluating the ego strength of an angry, deprived,   18.____
mistreated, frustrated, evasive client is the client's ability to

    A. verbalize his problems
    B. redirect his anger
    C. form a relationship with an accepting worker
    D. hold a job

19. When a worker, in his first interview with a parent, tries to take down a developmental   19.____
history of a boy, he usually gets many meaningless answers, such as *It was normal* or
I don't remember.
The worker should realize that

    A. this information is inaccurate and should be disregarded
    B. the parent is under stress at first, and should be able to give more factual informa-
       tion later
    C. the parent purposely is withholding valuable information about the boy
    D. the parent must be told that if he cannot cooperate he cannot be helped

20. One of the workers under your supervision is puzzled as to why a mother she was work-   20.____
ing with broke off contacts prermaturely. When you read the record of this mother, you
learn that she had become overdependent upon the worker before suddenly stopping
her visits.
In the supervisory conference, you should help the worker to understand that this type
of client

    A. is flighty, evasive, and has low reality testing
    B. is in need of deep psychotherapy
    C. is defending herself against this overdependence
    D. needs the chance to test her limits with an accepting person

21. When a worker is troubled because youths in his group ask him personal questions and he does not know how to answer them, as unit supervisor it would be BEST for you to advise the worker to   21.____

    A. interrogate the youths in detail about the reasons behind the questions
    B. tell the youths all they want to know, so that the worker appears friendly and human
    C. give a frank, brief, truthful answer and then immediately redirect the youths back to their own problems
    D. point out to the youths that the worker's personal life is not their business

22. Psychiatrists are usually concerned with the total functioning and integration of the human personality. Caseworkers usually concentrate on   22.____

    A. the same thing, but for shorter periods of time
    B. the same thing, but without prescribing medication
    C. helping the client to deal with the presenting problem
    D. all of the above

23. Some people feel that by cutting down temptations and stimuli, delinquency can be substantially decreased. Specific measures are curfews, eliminating the cruder forms of violence from the mass media, reducing the number of sexually stimulating publications available to youth, keeping down teenagers' resources for obtaining liquor, increasing recreational facilities, etc. The STRONGEST flaw in this approach is that   23.____

    A. it is not fair to non-delinquents
    B. it would not seriously affect the hard-core delinquent
    C. the community is not yet prepared for it
    D. it needs more time to prove itself

24. A COMMON error made by youth workers who are beginning to find out about the influence of unconscious desires and emotions on human behavior is to   24.____

    A. probe the client unnecessarily
    B. become over-assured that they can solve the client's problem
    C. slow up the pace of the interview
    D. look for the proper treatment method based on the client's neurosis

25. A basic technique which is used to obtain knowledge of the problem to be solved and sufficient understanding of the troubled person and of the situation, so that the problem can be solved effectively, is known as   25.____

    A. psychosomatics   B. interviewing
    C. recording   D. supervisory conferences

26. Which of the following is a CORRECT definition of the term *acceptance* as used in social work?   26.____

    A. A decision made at intake to accept the client as a case for the agency to handle
    B. The concept that the worker does not pass judgment on the client's behavior
    C. The concept of a positive and active understanding by the worker of the feelings a client expresses through his behavior
    D. Communication to the client that the worker does not condone and accept his anti-social behavior

27. Beginning youth workers are usually informed in a training session that they should be non-judgmental, should not become dependent on the client's liking them, and should not become angry. However, in an attempt to suppress these feelings, workers often behave in a stilted and artificial manner with clients.
As a supervisor, you should help your workers

    A. seek counseling to help them understand their angry feelings
    B. realize that they were not yet ready for that type of training
    C. understand that this artificiality will soon pass by as easily as it came
    D. recognize the naturalness of these feelings and learn to control their expression

27.____

28. A worker in the unit under your supervision has a youth in his group who has developed a strong antagonism toward him. You can find nothing that the worker has done to arouse such antagonism in the youth.
This antagonism is probably due to

    A. restrictions imposed on the client by the agency
    B. factors deeply hidden in the client's personality
    C. the youth's feeling of guilt because he has withheld information from the worker
    D. the fact that the worker may have promised the youth too much

28.____

29. The development of an emotional rapport, positive or negative, between the client and the worker is not abnormal, but inevitable. Sometimes the feelings that develop as a result of this rapport become excessively intense.
In those instances, the worker should

    A. request that the client be given another worker
    B. control the nature and intensity of the feelings
    C. ignore the feelings, which will disappear soon
    D. confront the client with the inappropriateness of these feelings

29.____

30. In social work, when we talk of ambivalence, we mean that the

    A. social worker refrains from imposing his moral judgments on the client
    B. supervisor assists the worker in understanding the psychological causes for client's behavior
    C. client has conflicting interests, desires, and emotions
    D. client is seeking someone who will understand the subjective reasons for his behavior

30.____

31. Although we can judge statements about objectively verifiable matters to be true or false, we are not similarly justified in passing judgments on subjective attitudes. This statement BEST explains the rationale behind the social work principle of

    A. empathy   B. self-awareness
    C. non-judgmentality   D. confidentiality

31.____

32. A psychological factor that explains why generally lawabiding individuals can become a part of a violent crowd is

    A. the deep urge for destruction and violence inherent in man
    B. the anonymity of the group would allow individuals to yield to restrained instincts
    C. that there is force in numbers, decreasing the likelihood of personal injury
    D. that man is basically a *herd animal,* so the mob is our natural environment

32.____

33. When you have learned that one of your workers has organized a protest, you should advise him to

    33._____

    A. be aware that the group may not be able to defend themselves against the police
    B. alert the community to distract the police to another area
    C. call off the protest because of the probability of danger
    D. take precautions with his group in order to be sure that the protest will be orderly

34. Some local merchants are disturbed because they feel that a group of boys who *hang on the corner* will develop into a delinquent gang. They invite you, the unit supervisor, to address them at a meeting in order to describe the characteristics of delinquent gangs to them.
In your talk to these merchants, you should

    34._____

    A. describe how delinquent gangs make a career of hanging around, have a blind loyalty among members, and see destruction as their way of hitting back at society
    B. advise them to call off the meeting because the delinquent gang as such has disappeared
    C. assure them that they should not be concerned because you have a worker in that area who has this group under surveillance
    D. contact your area administrator because this involves a relationship with the community that is not on your level of responsibility

35. According to the REPORT OF THE NATIONAL ADVISORY COMMITTEE ON CIVIL DISORDERS, riots are dramatic forms of protest expressing

    35._____

    A. hostility to government or private institutions
    B. undefined but real frustrations
    C. anger at the failure of society to provide certain groups with adequate opportunities
    D. all of the above

36. Many neighborhoods seem to develop a subculture in which forms of criminal and delinquent behavior and values are accepted as norms.
If the unit area happens to be in one of these neighborhoods, the unit supervisor would be BEST advised to keep in mind that

    36._____

    A. we know less about changing subcultures than we know about influencing groups and individuals
    B. it is easier to change subcultures than to influence groups and individuals
    C. subcultures are simple to identify, and helping the members to resolve their problems is comparatively easy
    D. this is only a theory and, therefore, should not influence the functioning of the unit office

37. The neighborhood drug abuse prevention network of the Addiction Services Agency is a series of broad-based community groups called

    37._____

    A. CARE AND AWARE   B. EVIL AND WEAK
    C. RARE AND AWARE   D. NACE AND CARE

38. An agency whose sole purpose is to fight addiction through a comprehensive prevention and rehabilitation program is

    A. Daytop Village
    B. Narcotics Addiction Control Commission
    C. Addiction Services Agency
    D. Phoenix House

38.____

39. Agencies which have been traditionally used by the Youth Services Agency for the purpose of sponsoring approved group programs to help youth improve their behavior are:

    A. Madison-Felicia, Vocational Advisory Service, Catholic Youth Organization, United Neighborhood Houses, Federation Employment and Guidance Service, Community Centers
    B. Office of Economic Opportunity, Catholic Youth Organization, Police Athletic League, Federation Employment and Guidance Service, Vocational Advisory Service, Jewish Family Service, Federation of Protestant Welfare Agencies
    C. Catholic Youth Organization, United Neighborhood Houses, Young Men's Christian Association, Protestant Council, Police Athletic League, Builders For the Family and Youth
    D. Catholic Youth Organization, Young Men's Christian Association, Protestant Council, Police Athletic League, Office of Economic Opportunity, Builders For Family and Youth, Vocational Advisory Service

39.____

40. Agencies that are used by Youth Services Agency to provide individual casework treatment services for Youth Services Agency clients who need individual therapy for deep-seated problems are:

    A. Jewish Family Services, State Division for Youth, Catholic Charities, Staten Island Family Service, Salvation Army, Community Education
    B. Big Brothers, Catholic Charities, Jewish Board of Guardians, Jewish Family Services, Salvation Army
    C. Catholic Youth Organization, Vocational Advisory Service, Melrose Center, Federation Employment and Guidance Service, United Neighborhood Houses
    D. Catholic Charities, Jewish Family Service, Vocational Foundation, Vermont Program, Big Brothers, Boys' Harbor, Salvation Army

40.____

41. The Departments that make up the Human Resources Administration are:

    A. Manpower and Career Development, Office of Economic Opportunity, Commission on Civil Disorders, Youth Services Agency, Addiction Services, Social Services, Community Development
    B. Manpower and Career Development Agency, Office of Economic Opportunity, Youth Services Agency, Addiction Services Agency, Department of Social Services, Commission on Human Rights, Community Volunteers
    C. Human Resources Administration Central Staff, Man power and Career Development Agency, Community Development Agency, Department of Social Services, Youth Services Agency, Addiction Services Agency, Office of Education Affairs
    D. Human Resources Administration Central Staff, Manpower and Career Development Agency, Department of Social Services, Youth Services Agency, Addiction Services Agency, Office of Economic Opportunity, Commission on Human Rights

41.____

42. A Youth Services Agency project that was developed in 1968 in response to the findings   42.____
of the National Advisory Commission on Civil Disorders (Kerner-Lindsay Report) and
which was designed to develop and demonstrate model approaches to engender interra-
cial understanding between teenagers is the

    A. Youth Opportunity Center
    B. Demonstration and Training Unit
    C. Interdepartmental Neighborhood Service Center
    D. Vermont Project

43. Which one of the following is mandated to provide services to the poverty-stricken, to   43.____
improve the quality of these services and the methods of delivering them, to carry out the
legal commitment to the poor, and to help the poor to help themselves?

    A. Office of Economic Opportunity
    B. Environmental Resources Administration
    C. Community Action Program
    D. Model Cities Program

44. An indication of mature behavior to be sought for in the client and encouraged by the   44.____
youth worker is the

    A. ability to become involved in issues of racism, urban life, and human rights
    B. development of some controls over the impulse to act out
    C. formulation of definite and specific goals in careers
    D. steady, consistent pattern of behavior that is relatively free of ambivalent feelings

45. That point in human development which marks a person's passage into adolescence is   45.____
known as

    A. maturity   B. the Oedipal stage
    C. the genital stage   D. puberty

46. An important factor to remember about the mental, physical, social, and emotional   46.____
growth of an adolescent is that the

    A. pace is uneven and individual
    B. pace is relatively even
    C. rate of growth is predictable
    D. growth has no special pattern

47. Adolescents are more likely to understand the concrete and the specific, rather than gen-   47.____
eral ideas like justice, honesty, love, etc.
The implication of this concept for the unit supervisor in guiding his staff is

    A. that programming should include recreation, job counseling, school help, and visits
at times of crisis
    B. the necessity to make sure that the programs use a large part of their budget for
treats for the youth
    C. to be sure the staff is directing much of their energy into pointing up the importance
of these general concepts
    D. to help the youths understand that life has taught them to be mistrustful

48. The theory of juvenile delinquency that traces much of delinquency back to failures in family relationships during the early years of childhood, and to continuing family difficulties, offers help to the youth worker in

    A. forming a general picture of the typical delinquent
    B. understanding that fighting is one of the best ways to rise to the top
    C. identifying normal growth needs of adolescents and the obstacles against healthy maturity
    D. realizing that delinquents are children at heart and are best treated as children

48.____

49. The theory of juvenile delinquency which holds that youths from minority groups turn to anti-social behavior when they feel that their access to social, educational, and economic opportunities in legal and approved ways is blocked has had a strong impact on the establishment of agencies like the

    A. Job Corps
    B. Community Development Agency
    C. Youth Board of the 1950's
    D. Addiction Services Agency

49.____

50. Which of the following is a descriptive term for a client who is resistive, breaks appointments, withholds information, beclouds issues, relates to others in a primitive, often distorted, fashion, and acts out his wishes and conflicts in his contact with the worker?

    A. Psychotic
    B. Narcotics addict
    C. Schizophrenic
    D. Character disorder

50.____

KEY (CORRECT ANSWERS)

1. A	11. A	21. C	31. C	41. C
2. B	12. D	22. C	32. B	42. D
3. A	13. B	23. B	33. D	43. A
4. B	14. B	24. A	34. A	44. B
5. B	15. A	25. B	35. D	45. D
6. C	16. A	26. C	36. A	46. A
7. A	17. B	27. D	37. C	47. A
8. B	18. C	28. B	38. C	48. C
9. A	19. B	29. B	39. C	49. A
10. A	20. C	30. C	40. B	50. D

TEST 2

DIRECTIONS: Each question or incomplete statement is followed by several suggested answers or completions. Select the one that BEST answers the question or completes the statement. *PRINT THE LETTER OF THE CORRECT ANSWER IN THE SPACE AT THE RIGHT.*

1. Adolescents who become involved in delinquent behavior are usually angry or frustrated a large part of their time. Conscious awareness of the intensity of their needs makes them feel weak.
   For this reason, they frequently

   A. are easier to work with
   B. prefer strong male youth workers
   C. need to be controlled and disciplined
   D. have to show the world they don't care what happens

   1.____

2. Sociologists and behavioral scientists provided the ideas of cohesion, conflict, competition, cooperation, authority, leadership, and stratification that are clearly manifested in

   A. supervision   B. addiction
   C. group behavior   D. casework therapy

   2.____

3. The one of the following causes of juvenile delinquency among sub-lower class youth which has been given increased attention in recent years is the

   A. prevalence of the one-parent family
   B. failure of family relationships in the early years
   C. blockage of educational, vocational, and social opportunities
   D. emotional problems and psychiatric disorders of youth

   3.____

4. A high-ranking official recently stated that some youths have made suicide attempts in detention centers so that they would be transferred from the detention centers to hospitals.
   If the workers in a unit should bring this topic up for discussion in a staff meeting, the supervisor should

   A. instruct workers to inform the youths of the area about this method of getting out of a detention center
   B. have a worker visit a youth in detention in order to observe and report back to the unit so that a demonstration can be organized
   C. assign different workers to study various aspects of the problem in order to plan an intelligent, informed discussion
   D. point out that the worker does not directly become involved with this problem, and direct the discussion to a more pertinent topic

   4.____

5. The MOST significant characteristics of the daily lives of alienated youths can be described as

   A. their days are aimless, disorganized, and unproductive
   B. they spend most of their time in antisocial activity
   C. they spend a good portion of their time seeking a means of earning money
   D. they concentrate most of their energies on actingout

   5.____

6. A young man drops into the office to request help in finding a job. While he is waiting to   6.____
    see the office coverage worker, you notice he is nervous, sweating, yawning, and con-
    stantly blowing his nose.
    As a unit supervisor, you should

    A. overlook this because the youth is probably worried about getting a job, and is dirty
        and tired
    B. feel assured that the worker will observe this also and handle it in the best possible
        way
    C. advise the worker of your observations, and discuss the possible causes of this
        behavior with the worker
    D. do none of the above

7. The *battered child syndrome* is reported to be one of the most difficult problems facing   7.____
    health officials.
    When a worker knows of a case of a boy being severely abused physically by his par-
    ents, the supervisor should advise the worker to

    A. discuss this with a psychiatrist to find out why the parent is abusing the child
    B. tell the child to stay away from the parents as much as possible
    C. try to talk to the parents to help them see what they are doing wrong
    D. report the situation to the Bureau of Child Welfare of the Department of Social Ser-
        vices

8. Ghetto youth today present symptoms of delinquent behavior that are in many ways   8.____
    more disruptive than those of the anti-social gang members of the 1950's. Some of these
    symptoms are

    A. alienation, school drop-outs, drug addiction, loosely formed cliques
    B. interracial conflicts, community violence, few family ties, teenage drifters, and pan-
        handlers
    C. promiscuity, alcoholism, vandalism, homosexuality, venereal disease
    D. all of the above

9. A psychological factor that tends to make the spread of drug abuse today easier among   9.____
    siblings in a family is the

    A. necessity for drug users to seduce others to join them
    B. need of siblings to rebel against parents
    C. fact that siblings can more easily *cover* for each other
    D. fact that older siblings can force younger siblings to take drugs

10. A parent complains to a worker that her teenage son is hanging around with a *bad*   10.____
    bunch, that money is strangely missing from the house lately, that his eating habits have
    changed, and that he spends long periods of time alone.
    When the worker discusses this with the unit supervisor, the supervisor should

    A. interview the parent as soon as possible to get more precise information
    B. advise the worker to refer the parent to a doctor to have her son examined
    C. help the worker to be supportive to the parent and try to make contact with the son
    D. assure him the parent is just jumpy over the drug scare and there is probably
        another explanation for the boy's behavior

11. A worker reports that the youths in his area think that *blowing pot* is all right because   11.____
marijuana is not addictive, is harmless in small doses, and is far less dangerous than
alcohol. The worker asks your help to talk the kids out of *blowing pot.*
You, as unit supervisor, should

  A. advise the worker to refer the youths to the nearest, best drug rehabilitation
     resource
  B. give the worker enough literature so the youths could learn more about the situa-
     tion
  C. assure the worker that these facts are true
  D. help the worker to involve the youths in constructive group activities

12. It is important for the youth worker to understand that the adolescent's FIRST loyalty   12.____
belongs to his

  A. peer group   B. siblings
  C. parents   D. best friend

13. One of the workers in a unit office reports that he is having some difficulty with his group   13.____
of youths. It is apparent that the youth leader of the group is seriously disturbed.
The BEST action for the worker to take FIRST is to

  A. try to redirect the leader's activities into more constructive channels
  B. help the group select a leader who is more psychologically sound
  C. take steps to have the leader removed from the community into a setting where he
     can get psychiatric help
  D. show this leader where his behavior is hurting the group so that he can change his
     behavior

14. The pleasurable effect produced by heroin is the   14.____

  A. feeling of excitement and energy
  B. expansion of sense perceptions
  C. feeling of relaxation, sociability, and good humor
  D. suppression of fears, tensions, and anxieties

15. The many rumors that spread throughout the Youth Services Agency are harmful to the   15.____
morale of the staff because they result in worry, suspicion, mistrust, and uncertainty. The
BEST way the unit supervisor can stop a rumor is to

  A. disregard it
  B. deny it
  C. start a different one
  D. give the staff the true facts

16. Parental rejection and neglect damage the personality of the developing child, and orient   16.____
the child toward his agemates in the neighborhood.
This statement would BEST describe the mechanism that leads to

  A. delinquency in urban industrial areas
  B. the establishment of neighborhood clubs
  C. the generation gap
  D. drug addiction

17. Many young people are introduced to drugs by friends. Youths don't like to be called   17._____
    chicken, they like to be *hip* like the rest, and they have to be a part of something.
    When a worker asks for your guidance on handling one of his youths who is being
    pressured into getting *high* by his friends, as the unit supervisor, you should help the
    worker

    A. gradually move this youth into another group of youths who are *straight*
    B. make the worker realize this is his problem, in his area, and that he must work it out
    the best way
    C. involve this youth and his group of friends in the programs and activities of the unit
    D. tell the youth he must work this out himself

18. Youth workers must help angry alienated adolescents to learn how to   18._____

    A. control their anger by learning when it's worthwhile to get angry
    B. suppress their angry feelings
    C. realize that anger is an unconscious emotion
    D. take part in aggressive demonstrations and takeovers

19. Of the following, an IMPORTANT reason why certain youths are stereotyped by the   19._____
    police and are therefore treated unfairly by them is that

    A. delinquent youths deserve to be treated more severely because they cause trouble
    for others
    B. these are only allegations and rhetoric made up by revolutionary elements who are
    hostile to the police
    C. the prevalence of *turnstile justice* results in hasty judgments by the police
    D. police officers in the field have no immediate data concerning the youths' back-
    grounds and react to their behavior at the moment

20. Group approaches are COMMONLY used for   20._____

    A. encounter, discussion, training, and administration
    B. education, counseling, therapy, and recreation
    C. counseling, recreation, catharsis, and crisis intervention
    D. competition, leadership, administration, and training

21. A worker under your supervision is having difficulty reaching some of the youths he is   21._____
    working with on a one-to-one basis. The recording on these youths shows that they have
    had little opportunity for healthy interpersonal relations.
    You should advise this worker to

    A. involve these youths in group counseling in order to help them overcome their
    reluctance in sharing experiences with another person
    B. refer these youths for psychiatric services because they are not likely to be
    reached by a youth worker
    C. assign these youths to Big Brothers or Big Sisters because they need to share a
    normal family experience
    D. give these youths more time to get to know and trust the worker

22. Planning, organization, methods, direction, coordination, budget and fiscal management, public relations, personnel administration, training, and supervision are the ESSENTIAL elements of

    A. group psychotherapy   B. ego-oriented casework
    C. consultation   D. administration

22._____

23. If a supervisor is unaware of a new worker's limitations and makes demands which are beyond the worker's capabilities, this will

    A. undermine the worker's confidence in functioning up to the limit of his actual capacities
    B. provide an incentive for the worker to further his training and improve services
    C. demonstrate the need for the agency to provide better orientation and in-service training for staff
    D. encourage the worker to function at a level higher than his present capacities

23._____

24. A high government official has announced: *We're looking for possible consolidation of services, for overlapping, for frills, for some built-in bureacratic procedures that have been kind of historic but that no one has ever taken a long look at to see if time and technology have made them obsolete.*
For the unit supervisor, the implication of this statement is that it is his responsibility to

    A. ignore this announcement since it pertains to matters beyond his responsibility
    B. report all matters of bureaucratic inefficiency directly to this high government official
    C. inform his workers at a staff meeting that there will be no funds for programs for the next few months
    D. try to involve the staff in a realistic reappraisal of the unit's program and discuss suggestions for cutbacks with the area administrator

24._____

25. Assume that you are a new unit supervisor in the Youth Services Agency and your workers bring many grievances to your attention.
The BEST way for you, the supervisor, to reduce grievances in your unit is to

    A. have the workers submit fully documented written grievances
    B. consider each grievance seriously and eliminate the cause if possible
    C. make workers realize that grievances reflect their immaturity and rejection of authority
    D. refer the workers' grievances to the area Administrator

25._____

26. Of the following, BASIC subject areas to be discussed in staff conferences are:

    A. Job responsibilities, agency structure, social work concepts, needs and resources of people
    B. Case-studying, interviewing, individual growth and development, sources of information other than the client
    C. Community resources, work organization, child welfare services, and standards of performance
    D. All of the above

26._____

27. The discussion method in teaching provides a way to help staff integrate knowledge and thus make it available for application to day-to-day work.
To help workers integrate knowledge and develop skill is an IMPORTANT aspect of

    A. professional training
    B. memos, directives, and position papers
    C. staff and individual conferences
    D. job descriptions

27.____

28. The subjects of discussion in staff meetings cannot be isolated from what the unit supervisor

    A. thinks is most important
    B. reads in books, journals, etc.
    C. hears at supervisors' meetings
    D. discusses in individual conferences

28.____

29. Interplay between persons appears to speed up the learning process; discussion of the material provides an opportunity for a sharing of knowledge and experience and allows for a testing out of new ideas and application of theory.
These are the objectives for

    A. Sensitivity Training
    B. T-Groups
    C. Staff Conferences
    D. Administrative Training

29.____

30. A leadership which aims to develop the individual staff member's skill and knowledge, and to direct activities of the staff in such a way as to bring about improvements in the agency's services given to the client. This is a description of GOOD

    A. staff development
    B. psychological direction
    C. public accountability
    D. supervision

30.____

31. In addition to familiarity with techniques in administrative planning and professional knowledge, the MOST important element in good supervision in a social agency is skill in

    A. office management
    B. human relations
    C. business methods
    D. psychological evaluation

31.____

32. If an agency does not have clear and specific unit and job functions, the MOST probable result will be

    A. a gross breakdown in services
    B. gaps and overlaps in responsibility and authority
    C. an inability to function according to the city charter
    D. a violation of the union contractual agreement

32.____

33. The one of the following which is the MOST important thing for a unit supervisor to keep in mind regarding the organizational structure of his unit is the

    A. preparation of time sheets and monthly reports
    B. two-way communication and maximum delegation
    C. geometric executive relationships
    D. critiques and controls

33.____

34. Budget and fiscal management is one essential practice of administration. A unit supervisor should see budgeting and fiscal management as a

    A. planning instrument
    B. fiscal control
    C. mandate from the civil service commission
    D. prerequisite of a union contractual agreement

34.____

35. Public relations with the community is one of the responsibilities of the unit supervisor. Good public relations means

    A. organizing the community to put pressure on officials in behalf of the agency
    B. getting reports from workers about the malcontents in the community and dealing with them in a diplomatic manner
    C. assuring the community that the unit will provide staff to problem areas
    D. getting understanding and cooperation from the community with which the agency is concerned

35.____

36. Problems and misunderstandings that arise from the lack of effective intraorganizational communication are apparent in many organizations.
Of the following, the means to be employed by the unit supervisor to establish effective communication are

    A. supervisory and staff conferences
    B. manuals, bulletins, and periodic reports
    C. bulletin boards, memos, and unit newsletters
    D. all of the above

36.____

37. A personnel problem facing supervisors in public service more than in private industry is

    A. union management and negotiation
    B. budget and fiscal control
    C. systematic selection and tenure
    D. advisory boards and political connections

37.____

38. Which of the following three types of records are COMMON to most social agencies?

    A. Administrative, budgetary, and case
    B. Administrative, statistical, and case
    C. Administrative, budgetary, and statistical
    D. Budgetary, statistical, and case

38.____

39. Even after several supervisory conferences on a case, a worker in your unit seems not to be giving effective help. In a burst of anger, the worker tells a coworker that the supervisor expects him to learn in a short time what the supervisor has taken years to learn. Of the following, the BEST description of the supervisory relationship here is that the

    A. supervisor is so intent on seeing that the necessary service is given that he is unaware of the worker's inability to perform the service
    B. worker's behavior shows that he is too immature to be working in such a difficult field

39.____

C. worker is unaware of casework principles and techniques and their application to such a difficult case

D. supervisor is unable to give the worker effective guidance in the supervisory conference, which indicates that the worker needs academic professional training

40. The one of the following which is NOT an essential ingredient of a good staff development and training program
is that it should

    40.____

A. include all members of the agency
B. meet the specific needs of the staff in relation to their job responsibilities
C. be a continuing process
D. give out the necessary rules and regulations of the agency

41. One of the areas in which consultation differs from supervision is that consultation

    41.____

A. is not in the direct administrative line of authority
B. is offered by someone skilled in a specific area
C. relates to procedure rather than function
D. requires special training

42. The supervisor should make sure the unit office keeps records about the youths it serves and their families since these records help in diagnosing and understanding the problems.
Of the following, as the PRIMARY source of information for case records, the workers should use

    42.____

A. reports from psychiatrists, doctors, etc.
B. all other agencies involved with the family
C. teachers, friends, local indigenous leaders
D. the parents and the youths themselves

43. Statistical records are needed for planning, research, and accountability although many workers feel that statistics are dull and boring. On the unit level, statistics can come alive when they are

    43.____

A. recorded in non-technical language
B. compiled by the unit expert in mathematics
C. collected selectively and used against a background knowledge of the community
D. elaborate, detailed, and accurate

44. With the passage of time, case records

    44.____

A. become more valuable
B. decline in usefulness
C. produce more information
D. become cumulative records

45. In general, the purpose of a case record is to

    45.____

A. improve staff training and development
B. make statistics pertinent and real
C. provide data for research
D. further professional service to a client

46. A unit supervisor finds after an intensive in-service training course in case recording that   46.____
his workers tend to postpone their recording and summaries.
The MOST likely explanation for this is that

    A. recording is not valuable enough to waste that amount of time on
    B. sufficient leadership was not given in the development of case records
    C. the workers are too busy in the field to have time to record
    D. the latest trend in social work is towards shorter records

47. A unit supervisor who has fewer youth workers in his unit than he can supervise effec-   47.____
tively will be likely to

    A. make his staff overdependent on him
    B. lack the desire to train his workers effectively
    C. confuse his staff because of lack of direction
    D. supervise his staff too closely

48. The one of the following which is MOST likely to be seriously impaired as a result of poor   48.____
supervision is the

    A. attitude of youth workers
    B. area of inter-departmental relations
    C. maintenance of case records and reports
    D. staff training and development program

49. It is generally good practice for the supervisor to ask for the opinions of his staff mem-   49.____
bers before taking action affecting them.
The GREATEST disadvantage of following this principle when changing schedules or
assignments is that staff may

    A. believe that the supervisor is unable to make his own decisions
    B. take advantage of the opportunity to present grievances during the discussion
    C. be resentful if their suggestions are not accepted
    D. suggest the same action as the supervisor had planned to take

50. The expansion of community relations or human relations units is a development result-   50.____
ing from the ghetto riots of the past few years.
The MOST important function such a unit can perform is to

    A. preach brotherhood and racial equality
    B. serve as a means for local city agency officials to develop city policy in accordance
with local needs
    C. serve as a means of communication between people with grievances and policy
makers who can take action
    D. give awards to prominent citizens who have promoted inter-racial understanding

———

KEY (CORRECT ANSWERS)

1.	D	11.	D	21.	A	31.	B	41.	A
2.	C	12.	A	22.	D	32.	B	42.	D
3.	C	13.	C	23.	A	33.	B	43.	C
4.	C	14.	D	24.	D	34.	A	44.	B
5.	A	15.	D	25.	B	35.	D	45.	D
6.	C	16.	A	26.	D	36.	D	46.	B
7.	D	17.	C	27.	C	37.	C	47.	D
8.	D	18.	A	28.	D	38.	B	48.	A
9.	A	19.	D	29.	C	39.	A	49.	C
10.	C	20.	B	30.	D	40.	A	50.	C

———

EXAMINATION SECTION
TEST 1

DIRECTIONS: Each question or incomplete statement is followed by several suggested answers or completions. Select the one that BEST answers the question or completes the statement. *PRINT THE LETTER OF THE CORRECT ANSWER IN THE SPACE AT THE RIGHT.*

1. The statement that the youth worker may be used by the members of his gang group as a *role model* means MOST NEARLY that the members may

    A. adopt the worker's behavior, attitudes, and beliefs as their own standards
    B. conceal their roles in the gang from the worker in order to gain his acceptance and trust
    C. test the worker by *acting out* on purpose
    D. conceal their roles in the gang from the worker in order to confuse him

1.____

2. Which of the following statements about the categories of gang members is CORRECT?
A

    A. peripheral member does not participate in gang conflict with core members
    B. core member is defined as a leader of the gang
    C. peripheral member is an informal gang leader
    D. core member is a full-fledged, accepted member of the gang

2.____

3. An uncooperative and antagonistic attitude among adult groups toward youth workers seeking to modify criminal patterns of behavior among youth gang groups is MOST likely to be prevalent in a neighborhood where

    A. efforts of youth-serving agencies long established in the community have produced no tangible results
    B. significant segments of the adult population engage in or support various types of criminal activity
    C. powerful middle-class elements of the population refuse to openly admit the existence of anti-social youth groups, for fear of giving the neighborhood a bad reputation
    D. behavior patterns of gang groups are extremely aggressive and destructive of life and property in the neighborhood

3.____

4. The characteristics of the groups to be served are a major consideration in developing programs for delinquent youth.
In general, it has been found that the anti-social acts of juvenile delinquents in neighborhoods that are lowest on the socio-economic scale, compared to the anti-social acts of juvenile delinquents in less deprived areas, are

    A. more aggressive   B. less aggressive
    C. more organized   D. easier to control

4.____

5. The peer group is even more important for the delinquent adolescent who comes from a severely disadvantaged background than for the comparatively normal middle-class adolescent, MAINLY because the peer group provides the delinquent adolescent with

    A. protection from a usually extreme sense of failure resulting from defective family, school, and other relationships

5.____

B. ways of obtaining needed funds by participating with their peers in such anti-social acts as muggings, robbery, and petty larceny

C. opportunities to participate in recreational activities that are usually available only to middle-class adolescents

D. access to preparation for realistic adult goals in such legitimate occupations as construction worker, dock worker, or other unskilled and semi-skilled jobs

6. A street-based youth services program is more exposed to community view and evaluation than a program based in a community center or other indoor meeting place. Therefore, there is greater risk of community disapproval and loss of support.
Of the following, the BEST way to minimize this risk is for the agency sponsoring a street-based program to

A. make every effort to withhold information from the community about such incidents as gang fights, homicides, and criminal activities involving youth

B. interpret the nature of the service to the community clearly and objectively, giving information about both negative and positive results of the program

C. arrange for neighborhood gang groups to congregate in their clubrooms wherever possible, so that their activities will not be exposed to view

D. insist that the police enforce strong punitive measures when gang groups commit anti-social acts that may cause community disapproval of a street-based program

6.____

7. Which of the following statements about differences in attitudes and reactions toward delinquent behavior is NOT valid?
Behavior

A. viewed as delinquent in a middle-class neighborhood may not be so regarded in a lower-class neighborhood

B. considered delinquent in one lower-class neighborhood may be regarded with less concern in another lower-class neighborhood

C. which a youth worker considers delinquent and attempts to change when he has established a positive relationship with a gang group would be handled differently during his early contacts with the group

D. which a youth worker considers delinquent and attempts to change during his early contacts with a gang group would be treated more leniently when he has established a positive relationship with the group

7.____

8. The area approach to street work is oriented more toward sociological theory than social work. It rests on the assumption that delinquent gangs reflect the normal strivings of groups of youngsters whose opportunities for *acceptable* behavior are limited.
The one of the following which is MOST likely to be the major emphasis of practitioners of the area approach to street work with youth is to

A. preserve the gang structure and provide intensive supportive counseling services to individual members and their families

B. undermine the gang structure and provide intensive supportive counseling services to members and their families

C. preserve the gang structure and provide more opportunities for gang members to channel their behavior into constructive activities

D. undermine the gang structure and channel the behavior of its members into more constructive activities

8.____

9. Research studies have demonstrated that the social health of a community is directly related to the

    A. opportunities available to its residents
    B. effectiveness of the police in the community
    C. number of social, agencies located in the community
    D. influence of community organizations and groups

    9._____

10. Because of the complexity of interacting forces contributing to the problems of the delinquent, the gang, and the community, the youth worker's efforts frequently meet with failure.
    It is, therefore, IMPORTANT for the supervisor to help his workers to concentrate their efforts with anti-social youth on

    A. attaining appropriate and often reasonably low levels of improvement
    B. helping mainly those group members who are most likely to profit from his attention
    C. protecting the community from the youths' destructive and anti-social acts
    D. referring the most seriously disturbed youths to agencies staffed by psychiatric professionals

    10._____

11. The PRIMARY concern of the youth worker who uses the group work approach with small gang groups would be the

    A. interrelationship of group members with each other, with their peers and with adults outside the group
    B. background of each group member in terms of his school, unemployment, and family problems
    C. nature and quality of the illegal activities engaged in by the members of the group
    D. attitudes expressed by local police agencies toward this type of approach with anti-social youths

    11._____

12. For a youth worker to support the efforts of a conventionally oriented subgroup of a gang to break away from the rest of the group would GENERALLY be

    A. *undesirable,* chiefly because the two groups will probably engage in a gang fight if they separate
    B. *desirable,* if the behavior of the largest number of the group members is highly deviant and anti-social
    C. *undesirable,* chiefly because the conventionally oriented subgroup will no longer be able to prevent the highly deviant members from engaging in antisocial activities
    D. *desirable,* if the larger group is cohesive and the behavior of its members is somewhat constructive

    12._____

13. A *vertical* group of gang members would be structured according to

    A. turf   B. ethnicity   C. age   D. leadership role

    13._____

14. In terms of helping the group, which of the following types of leadership would generally be considered MOST acceptable for a youth worker to use with a loosely structured, street-oriented group of youths?

    A. Laissez-faire   B. Manipulative   C. Democratic   D. Autocratic

    14._____

15. According to Richard A. Cloward and Lloyd E. Ohlin, in DELINQUENCY AND OPPOR-   15._____
    TUNITY, members of a retreatist sub-culture

    A. retreat during rumbles with members of other gangs
    B. are mainly involved in the use of drugs
    C. do not become involved in anti-social activities
    D. seek status through violent activities

16. Medical specialists and other health and community officials have reported that the   16._____
    recent resurgence of youth gangs and youth violence has been accompanied by a

    A. considerable increase in youthful drug addiction and -criminal activity involving
       drugs
    B. marked decrease in illegitimate pregnancies and requests for abortions from
       women's auxiliary gang members
    C. considerable increase in alcoholism and related illnesses and emergencies involv-
       ing ghetto youth
    D. marked decrease in overdose cases and other indications of narcotics use

17. An inexperienced youth worker assigned to a large gang group expresses concern to his   17._____
    supervisor about the possibility of gang conflict and doesn't know which of the members
    should be kept under closest surveillance.
    The supervisor should advise him that is is MOST important to give closest surveil-
    lance to the

    A. president   B. war counselor
    C. core members   D. peripheral members

18. The author of an early classic text on street gangs in Chicago is   18._____

    A. K.H. Rogers   B. Irving Spergel
    C. F.M. Thrasher   D. R.K. Merton

19. The members of an anti-social street gang who should be the objects of the MOST seri-   19._____
    ous concern to youth workers are those who characteristically

    A. show an inability to cope effectively with their own impulsive behavior
    B. behave in a friendly, over-solicitous and helpful manner
    C. act bossy and try to convince the worker to accede to their demands
    D. refuse to accept the worker's friendly overtures and offers of assistance

20. The special language used by members of adolescent street gangs typically reflects their   20._____
    roles as alienated youth in a delinquent subculture.
    The one of the following which is NOT a usual characteristic of their vocabulary is

    A. grandiosity
    B. identification with the underdog
    C. possession of values counter to the larger society
    D. denial of reality

21. Assume that it has been decided that the youth services agency will terminate services to the *Lightning Rods,* a gang group which has not been involved in *jitterbugging* for about two years. When the members, who have developed a strong attachment to their worker, learn that soon they will no longer have regular contact with him, they start to fight and become involved in other anti-social incidents again. As a result, the worker tells his supervisor that he believes he should continue his assignment with the group. The supervisor SHOULD advise the worker to

    21.____

    A. continue his services and so inform the group
    B. reassure the group that he will be available if needed, even though he will not see them regularly
    C. disregard the recent incidents, since this is the group's way of seeking attention
    D. make a sharp break with the group, and meet with him in order to discuss his apprehension about losing contact with these youths

22. A supervisor has a new worker whose records indicate that he has potential for becoming an excellent staff member. However, when the supervisor observes the worker in the field, he notices that the worker frequently holds back and seems uncertain in handling his group. When the supervisor talks to the worker about this in private, the worker explains that he hesitates because he is *afraid of doing the wrong thing.*
The BEST way for the supervisor to help this worker is to

    22.____

    A. assign him to another group until he gets more experience
    B. suggest to him that he would feel better if he had professional training
    C. give him reassurance and as much guidance as he needs
    D. go into the field with him to work with his youths so he can learn directly from him

23. Assume that, when a supervisor visits a gang group for the first time, the group reacts to the supervisor in an antagonistic and hostile manner.
It would be ADVISABLE for the supervisor to

    23.____

    A. stop visiting the group until he learns from their worker that they have a more positive attitude toward him
    B. discuss the situation with the assigned worker and direct him to call the group to a meeting in the unit office
    C. return to visit the group frequently, making friendly approaches until a better relationship is established
    D. take the group on a bus trip to Bear Mountain without their worker in order to foster a better relationship

24. Assume that a consultant, who has been brought in to review programs in a youth services agency unit, tells the supervisor that he has found that several workers have spent program money for their own personal needs. The supervisor should FIRST

    24.____

    A. recommend that the workers involved be brought up on charges
    B. realize that the consultant's findings may be biased, and take no further action until he hears from central office
    C. accept the consultant's findings, because the consultant has the ultimate responsibility
    D. review his records and discuss the findings with his staff, in order to determine the facts for himself

25. In the course of a field visit to a youth services agency unit, a supervisor learns that a youth worker has been involved sexually with one of the *debs* in his assigned group. Which of the following would be the MOST appropriate action for the supervisor to take?

    A. Suspend the worker immediately
    B. Allow the worker to continue with his assigned group until a hearing is arranged
    C. Confront the worker with his knowledge of the situation and assign him to the office pending further investigation
    D. Confer with the worker and explain that such an involvement will eventually adversely affect his relationship with the group

25.____

Questions 26-30.

DIRECTIONS: Questions 26 through 30 are based on the following example of a youth worker's incident report. The report consists of ten numbered sentences, some of which are not consistent with the principles of good report writing.

(1) On the evening of February 24, James and Larry, two members of the *Black Devils,* were entering with a bottle of wine in their hands. (2) It was unusually good wine for these boys to buy. (3) I told them to give me the bottle and they refused, and added that they wouldn't let anyone *put them out.* (4) I told them they were entitled to have a good time, but they could not do it the way they wanted; there were certain rules they had to observe. (5) At this point, James said he had seen me box at camp and suggested that Larry not accept my offer. (6) Then I said firmly that the admission fee did not give them the authority to tell me what to do. (7) I also told them that, if they thought I would fight them over such a matter, they were sadly mistaken. (8) I added, however, that we could go to the gym right now and settle it another way if they wished. (9) Larry immediately said that he was sorry, he had not understood the rules, and he did not want his quarter back. (10) On the other hand, they would not give up their bottle either, so they left the premises.

26. Only material that is relevant to the main thought of a report should be included. Which of the following sentences from the report contains material which is LEAST relevant to this report?
Sentence

    A. 2   B. 3   C. 8   D. 9

26.____

27. A good report should be arranged in logical order. Which of the following sentences from the report does NOT appear in its proper sequence in the report?
Sentence

    A. 3   B. 5   C. 7   D. 9

27.___

28. Reports should include all essential information.
Of the following, the MOST important fact that is missing from this report is

    A. who was involved in the incident
    B. how the incident was resolved
    C. when the incident took place
    D. where the incident took place

28.___

29. The MOST serious of the following faults commonly found in explanatory reports is 29.____

   A. use of slang terms B. excessive details
   C. personal bias D. redundancy

30. In reviewing a report he has prepared to submit to his superiors, a supervisor finds that 30.____
   his paragraphs are a typewritten page long and decides to make some revisions. Of the
   following, the MOST important question he should ask about each paragraph is:

   A. Are the words too lengthy?
   B. Is the idea under discussion too abstract?
   C. Is more than one central thought being expressed?
   D. Are the sentences too long?

KEY (CORRECT ANSWERS)

1.	A	16.	D
2.	D	17.	C
3.	B	18.	C
4.	A	19.	A
5.	A	20.	B
6.	B	21.	B
7.	D	22.	C
8.	C	23.	C
9.	A	24.	D
10.	A	25.	C
11.	A	26.	A
12.	B	27.	B
13.	C	28.	D
14.	C	29.	C
15.	B	30.	C

TEST 2

DIRECTIONS: Each question or incomplete statement is followed by several suggested answers or completions. Select the one that BEST answers the question or completes the statement. *PRINT THE LETTER OF THE CORRECT ANSWER IN THE SPACE AT THE RIGHT.*

1. Of the following, the factor that is MOST critical and MOST likely to influence the success of the youth worker's handling of aggression by gang group members is the

    A. time and place of the aggressive acts by the group members
    B. timing of the worker's action to curb the aggression
    C. number of group members taking part in the aggressive action
    D. availability of resources to distract the gang group members

1.____

2. When the leadership of a gang is highly negative or delinquent in nature, it is considered ADVISABLE for a worker who has a positive relationship with the group to

    A. assist the group to shift leadership from the delinquency oriented to the more conventionally oriented members
    B. attempt to oust the deviant leaders from the group
    C. give special attention to programs for the conventionally oriented members
    D. report the highly deviant leaders to the authorities in order to destroy their influence with the group

2.____

3. Of the following, the MOST important function of the central communications system in an area-based youth services unit is to permit the supervisor to

    A. learn where workers are in the field, and advise or direct them as to the most appropriate way of handling an emergency
    B. relay important information about unit activities and programs to higher-level personnel in the central office
    C. inform the community of the activities of the agency and its achievements in curbing delinquent behavior of neighborhood youth
    D. relay information about policies and procedures as well as routine matters to staff based in the field

3.____

4. Experts have criticized the use of the Glueck Juvenile Delinquency Prediction Table MAINLY because

    A. a child's personality changes during the various stages of growth
    B. statistics are irrelevant when applied to individuals
    C. personnel who use it may not be properly trained
    D. school personnel may not be objective with children identified as potentially delinquent

4.____

5. Under the present organization of the youth services agency, the basic unit of service is the

    A. central office
    B. technical assistance unit
    C. community planning district
    D. community board

5.____

6. The function of the *outreach* staff of the youth services agency is to   6.____

    A. provide professional casework services and in-service training to unit staff involved in referrals
    B. identify youths in the community with severe behavioral and psychological problems and refer them for professional help
    C. make contacts with community groups and agencies in order to help them administer their own programs
    D. provide youth with opportunities to take part in community planning and make suggestions for their own programs

7. A youth worker who wants to find out whether a youth in his group and his family are registered with other social and health agencies could get this information from the   7.____

    A. Community Service Society
    B. Social Service Exchange
    C. Contributors Information Bureau
    D. Council of Voluntary Agencies

8. Assume that the only guidelines used by a youth services agency staff member assigned to evaluate a contract agency were the contract agency's standards for administration, supervision, and programming.
Of the following, the MOST important guideline omitted by the evaluator relates to the contract agency's   8.____

    A. lower-level staff   B. physical facilities
    C. board of directors   D. other funding resources

9. The MOST important purpose of social program evaluation as it is carried out in the youth services agency is to   9.____

    A. justify current program operations
    B. provide an objective basis for reductions in program funding
    C. introduce youth services agency personnel to profes-sionals in contract agencies
    D. provide an objective basis for decision-making on programs which will provide effective services to youth

10. The one of the following which is NOT usually included as part of the consultation services provided by the youth services agency staff member assigned to evaluate a contract agency is giving   10.____

    A. opinion and advice on program content
    B. information on resources in the youth services agency and the community
    C. help with the formulation of program proposals
    D. in-service training to agency staff

Questions 11-15.

DIRECTIONS: Questions 11 through 15 are to be answered SOLELY on the basis of the following passage.

In an attempt to describe what is meant by a delinquent subculture, let us look at some delinquent activities. We usually assume that when people steal things, they steal because they want them to eat or wear or otherwise use them; or because they can sell them; or even - if we are given to a psychoanalytic turn of mind -because on some deep symbolic level the things stolen substitute or stand for something unconsciously desired but forbidden. However, most delinquent gang stealing has no such utilitarian motivation at all. Even where the value of the object stolen is itself a motivating consideration, the stolen sweets are often sweeter than those acquired by more legitimate and prosaic means. In homelier language, stealing *for the hell of it* and apart from considerations of gain and profit is a valued activity to which attaches glory, prowess, and profound satisfaction.

Similarly, many other delinquent activities are motivated mainly by an enjoyment in the distress of others and by a hostility toward non-gang peers as well as adults. Apart from the more dramatic manifestations in the form of gang wars, there is keen delight in terrorizing *good* children and in driving them from playgrounds and gyms for which the gang itself may have little use. The same spirit is evident in playing hooky and in misbehavior in school. The teacher and her rules are not merely to be evaded. They are to be flouted.

All this suggests that the delinquent subculture is not only a set of rules, a design for living which is different from or indifferent to or even in conflict with the norms of the *respectable* adult society. It actually takes its norms from the larger culture but turns them upside down. The delinquent's conduct is right, by the standards of his subculture, precisely because it is wrong by the standards of the larger culture.

11. Of the following, the MOST suitable title for the above passage is   11._____

    A. DIFFERENT KINDS OF DELINQUENT SUBCULTURES
    B. DELINQUENT HOSTILITY TOWARD NON-GANG PEERS
    C. METHODS OF DELINQUENT STEALING
    D. DELINQUENT STANDARDS AS REVEALED BY THEIR ACTIVITIES

12. It nay be inferred from the passage that MOST delinquent stealing is motivated by a   12._____

    A. need for food and clothing
    B. need for money to buy drugs
    C. desire for peer-approval
    D. symbolic identification of the thing stolen with hidden desires

13. The passage IMPLIES that an important reason why delinquents play hooky and misbe-   13._____
have in school is that the teachers

    A. represent *respectable* society
    B. are boring
    C. have not taught them the values of the adult society
    D. are too demanding

14. In the passage, the author's attitude toward delinquents is   14._____

    A. critical   B. objective
    C. overly sympathetic   D. confused

15. According to the passage, which of the following statements is CORRECT?   15.____

    A. Delinquents derive no satisfaction from stealing.
    B. Delinquents are not hostile toward someone without a reason.
    C. The common motive of many delinquent activities is a desire to frustrate others.
    D. The delinquent subculture shares its standards with the *respectable* adult culture.

Questions 16-18.

DIRECTIONS: Questions 16 through 18 are to be answered SOLELY on the basis of the following paragraph.

A fundamental part of the youth worker's role is changing the interaction patterns which already exist between the delinquent group and the representatives of key institutions in the community, e.g., the policeman, teacher, social worker, employer, parent, and storekeeper. This relationship, particularly its definitional character, is a *two-way* proposition. The offending youth or group will usually respond by fulfilling this prophecy. In the same way, the delinquent expects punishment or antagonistic treatment from officials and other representatives of middle class society; in turn, the adult concerned may act to fulfill the prophecy of the delinquent. Stereotyped patterns of expectation, both of the delinquents and those in contact with them, must be changed. The worker can be instrumental in changing these patterns.

16. Of the following, the MOST suitable title for the paragraph is   16.____

    A. WAYS TO PREDICT JUVENILE DELINQUENCY
    B. THE YOUTH WORKER'S ROLE IN CREATING STEREOTYPES
    C. THE YOUTH WORKER'S ROLE IN CHANGING STEREOTYPED PATTERNS OF EXPECTATION
    D. THE DESIRABILITY OF INTERACTION PATTERNS

17. According to the paragraph, a youth who misbehaves and is told by an agency worker that *his group is a menace to the community* would PROBABLY eventually respond by   17.____

    A. withdrawing into himself
    B. continuing to misbehave
    C. making a greater attempt to please
    D. acting indifferent

18. In this paragraph, the author's opinion about stereotypes is that they are   18.____

    A. *useful,* primarily because they are usually accurate
    B. *useful,* primarily because they make a quick response easier
    C. *harmful,* primarily because the adult community will be less aware of delinquents as a group
    D. *harmful,* primarily because they influence behavior

Questions 19-20.

DIRECTIONS: Questions 19 and 20 are to be answered SOLELY on the basis of the following paragraph.

A drug-user does not completely retreat from society. While a new user, he must begin participation in some group of old users in order to secure access to a steady supply of drugs. In the process, his readiness to engage in drug use, which stems from his personality and the social structure, is reinforced by new patterns of associations and values. The more the individual is caught in this web of associations, the more likely it is that he will persist in drug use, for he has become incorporated into a subculture that exerts control over his behavior. However, it is also true that the resulting tics among addicts are not as strong as those among participants in criminal and conflict subcultures. Addiction is in many ways an individualistic adaptation, for the *kick* is essentially a private experience. The compelling need for the drug is also a divisive force, for it leads to intense competition among addicts for money. Forces of this kind thus limit the relative cohesion which can develop among users.

19. According to the paragraph, the MAIN reason why new drug users associate with old users is a

    A. fear of the police   B. common hatred of society
    C. need to get drugs   D. dislike of being alone

19._____

20. According to the paragraph, which of the following statements is INCORRECT?

    A. Drug users encourage each other to continue taking drugs.
    B. Gangs that use drugs are more cohesive than other delinquent gangs.
    C. A youth's desire to use drugs stems from his personality as well as the social structure.
    D. Addicts get no more of a *kick* from using drugs in a group than alone.

20._____

21. The MOST appropriate of the following methods for a supervisor to use FIRST in order to become knowledgeable about a gang group assigned to one of his workers is to

    A. work with the group on the worker's scheduled days off
    B. read the worker's recordings and discuss the group with the worker in supervisory conferences
    C. observe the worker in the field as he interacts with group members
    D. accompany the group on trips and other programmed activities

21._____

22. Assume that a supervisor has been assigned to take workers into a community which is in an uproar as a result of a recent outbreak of gang conflict during which a youth was killed. There were no youth services agency units or street workers in this community previously. The supervisor SHOULD approach this situation by

    A. calling a meeting with representatives of all the gang groups in order to assess the situation and discuss possible ways of curbing the conflicts
    B. contacting the police precinct for information about the hangouts of the gangs
    C. assigning workers to contact gang groups and urge them to move their activities out of the neighborhood
    D. meeting with the neighborhood leaders, staff of community organizations and other social agencies to discuss the magnitude of the problem and to mobilize resources

22._____

23. As a result of longstanding resentment between two gangs covered by a supervisor's unit, a popular youth who belonged to a third gang group was shot to death by accident. How should the supervisor handle this crisis?

23._____

A. Immediately call a meeting of all the gang groups in the area to assess their feelings about the youth's death
B. Mobilize unit workers to cover as many groups as possible, in order to be able to monitor their movements and plans
C. Submit requests for buses to remove the two hostile groups from the area
D. Request assistance from members of neighborhood auxiliary police in the area

24. In the course of a field visit, a supervisor learns for the first time that a worker has been discussing a weekend trip to Philadelphia with his assigned group when several youths in the group come up to him and ask for his deci-sion on the trip.
The BEST course of action for the supervisor to take Would be to tell the youth that   24._____

A. he approves of the trip, so that the youths will not be frustrated
B. he disapproves of the trip, so that the worker will learn to request approval before getting the youths excited about a trip
C. the worker did not discuss the trip with him, but that the worker will have to make the decision anyway
D. he is still considering the trip, and will evaluate it later on its own merits

25. It is frequently difficult for a supervisor to convince youth workers assigned to street gangs of the importance of recording.
While training his workers in proper recording methods, the supervisor should empha-size that, of the following, the MOST important purpose of recording is to   25._____

A. evaluate progress made by groups and individual members
B. determine the effectiveness of the agency as a whole
C. identify flaws in on-going programs
D. plan future programs

Questions 26-30.

DIRECTIONS: In Questions 26 through 30, choose the lettered word or expression which is closest to the meaning of the first word or expression, *as used most frequently by street-oriented youths and members of youth gangs.* Do not try to give the usually accepted or dictionary definition of the word or expression.

26. wig out   26._____

A. shoplift clothes   B. engage in homosexuality
C. feel shocked   D. refuse to use drugs

27. dipple   27._____

A. cocaine user   B. former hippie
C. unit of drugs   D. nervous junkie

28. flaky   28._____

A. a little abnormal mentally
B. nervy
C. enjoyable
D. beaten to a pulp

29. wag tail

29.____

    A. succeed   B. conform   C. fool   D. inform

30. dolphins

30.____

    A. amphetamines   B. suspicious pushers
    C. methadone pills   D. pimps

KEY (CORRECT ANSWERS)

1.	B	16.	C
2.	A	17.	B
3.	A	18.	D
4.	D	19.	C
5.	C	20.	B
6.	B	21.	B
7.	B	22.	D
8.	A	23.	B
9.	D	24.	D
10.	D	25.	A
11.	D	26.	C
12.	C	27.	B
13.	A	28.	A
14.	B	29.	B
15.	C	30.	C

EXAMINATION SECTION
TEST 1

DIRECTIONS: Each question or incomplete statement is followed by several suggested answers or completions. Select the one that BEST answers the question or completes the statement. *PRINT THE LETTER OF THE CORRECT ANSWER IN THE SPACE AT THE RIGHT.*

1. The one of the following which CORRECTLY describes the general characteristics of a typical street gang is a

    A. loosely federated group of youths, who take part in occasional delinquent acts as well as social and recreational activities

    B. closely-attached clique of friends, who require approval of each new member by a committee of older members

    C. highly unstructured youth group with at least 100 members and several elected officers

    D. group composed of no more than 10 or 12 close friends who have all grown up on the same street

1.____

2. Of the following, a SIGNIFICANT difference between present-day youth gangs and the youth gangs of the 1950's is that gang members today

    A. are talking about solving such problems as housing, jobs, and getting off welfare

    B. are generally younger and less sophisticated

    C. use a language of their own

    D. are less likely to have criminal records

2.____

3. Statistics indicate that more delinquent acts are committed by youth who come from families of low socio-economic status than by middle- or upper-class youth. The one of the following which is GENERALLY considered to be an important reason for these statistics is that

    A. middle- and upper-class youth are protected by their parents' influence and are generally treated more leniently by police

    B. youth of lower socioeconomic status usually have weaker characters

    C. behavior considered to be a crime by lower-class families is not considered criminal by middle-class families

    D. middle- and upper-class youth are clever in concealing their illegal acts

3.____

4. Members of a minority group which experiences discrimination by a dominant group USUALLY react by

    A. seeking security by establishing social relationships with the dominant group

    B. choosing its leaders from the dominant group

    C. becoming more closely unified as a reaction to such discrimination

    D. becoming disorganized as individual members seek acceptance from the dominant group

4.____

5. Assume that, as a result of several recent gang killings, the newspapers have been editorializing about the evils of youth gangs, demanding that the police arrest gang leaders and members of street corner youth groups. Which of the following would be the MOST advisable action for the administration of a youth services agency to take in an attempt to relieve tension created by these newspaper articles?

    A. Order staff to work more intensively with their assigned groups and program them in activities outside of their neighborhoods

    B. Have the public relations office invite newsmen to tour the neighborhoods, describing the agency's work with gangs and the constructive aspects of group relationships

    C. Instruct workers to talk to members of youth gangs and order them not to *hang out* on street corners

    D. Instruct workers to talk to the police and describe to them the youth services agency's constructive work with youth groups

5.____

6. Research has shown that the MAJOR form of delinquency among street-oriented girls' gangs is

    A. petty theft, such as shoplifting

    B. sexual misbehavior, including promiscuity and prostitution

    C. helping boys' gangs in criminal activities

    D. violent attacks on other girls, or street muggings

6.____

7. Recent studies indicate that MOST youth gangs in low-income neighborhoods have

    A. a stable group of all-male members

    B. female members who take more passive roles than the male members

    C. an approximately equal number of male and female members

    D. definite goals which are formulated by the male members

7.____

8. A hospital would probably be a more favorable setting than a commercial laundry for a work project for disadvantaged youths, no matter what kind of work they are assigned to do, MAINLY because a hospital would

    A. be more likely to offer steady employment and fringe benefits

    B. expose youths with delinquent tendencies to fewer temptations

    C. give the youths more opportunity to become acquainted with adults who work at higher occupational levels

    D. be more likely to tolerate unacceptable behavior on the job

8.____

9. A suggestion has been made that the parents of delinquent youths, rather than the youths themselves, be brought into court for trial.
Of the following, the MOST forceful argument against this suggestion is that

    A. court action against the parents will lower their prestige in the eyes of their children

    B. parents cannot be considered responsible for the delinquent acts of their children

    C. court action against the parents will not cause the children to feel guilty for their acts

    D. juvenile delinquents cannot be helped to change their behavior unless they are made to feel fully responsible for their acts

9.____

10. Of the following, the MAIN reason why a worker has an important part to play in encour-   10.____
aging street-oriented youths to participate in education-work-training programs is that

    A. the worker is best qualified to provide needed information on available employment
    B. schools and other organizations might not be willing to refer youths with histories of
delinquent behavior to these programs
    C. street-oriented youths are not likely to be reached through schools and other orga-
nizations which usually make referrals to such programs
    D. the worker may be the only person who could provide prospective employers with
objective information about the youths

11. Of the following, the MAIN reason why membership in a peer group is of great impor-   11.____
tance to adolescents is that the peer group provides

    A. ways to achieve a meaningful social identity
    B. opportunity to cover up criminal activity
    C. protection from the police
    D. opportunity to *fight the system*

12. In general, it has been found that the lower the socio-economic level of its neighborhood,   12.____
the more likely a gang is to

    A. become involved in anti-social and violent activity
    B. benefit from participation in team sports
    C. have several members hung up on heroin
    D. suspect the worker to be a police informer

13. Research studies show that commitment of delinquent youth to correctional institutions,   13.____
juvenile homes, training schools, and other similar facilities has GENERALLY led to

    A. rehabilitation of the individual offender
    B. a high rate of return to these institutions
    C. a temporary decrease in delinquent behavior by fellow gang members
    D. an overall reduction in crime in the community

14. With regard to youthful offenders, statistics on arrests and court commitments of youth   14.____
tend to

    A. exaggerate the relative seriousness of crimes committed by juveniles
    B. give an accurate picture of the amount of juvenile delinquency
    C. exaggerate the total amount of juvenile delinquency
    D. underestimate the total amount of juvenile delinquency

15. It is generally considered desirable for the worker to make every effort to help youthful   15.____
delinquents to solve their problems while they are living in the community. However,
when a youth is consistently in trouble and is self-destructive, the BEST course of action
would be for the worker to

    A. try to stay with him as much as possible to provide supervision and keep him out of
trouble
    B. report him to the principal of his school
    C. support his being sent to a training school or other institution
    D. urge him to join a school athletic team, so that the coach can keep an eye on him

16. Because street youth groups vary widely in their makeup and patterns of behavior, it is important for the worker to   16._____

    A. work only with those groups that are prepared to come into a youth center and abide by its rules
    B. develop a single approach that can be applied to all gangs
    C. concentrate only on groups that are likely to benefit from help
    D. use varied approaches in order to suit the patterns of different groups and problem individuals

17. Voluntary social agencies based in disadvantaged neighborhoods often fail to meet the needs of the poor people living in the community.   17._____
Of the following, the MOST likely reason for such failure is

    A. lack of participation by the local poor in planning the programs of the agency
    B. inefficient administration of the agency
    C. inability of the local poor to contribute funds to the agency
    D. lack of interest on the part of the poor because of increased availability of public funds for local projects

18. A worker learns that the settlement house in his assigned area, which has a contract with the youth services agency and has agreed to provide services for all neighborhood youths, refuses to allow members of his group to use the center's facilities.   18._____
The FIRST step for the youth worker to take would be to

    A. call the director of the center and tell him firmly that he is under contract to serve all youths in the community
    B. find another community center for group meetings
    C. refer the matter to the agency contract department
    D. meet with the settlement director and determine the reason for excluding the group

19. One of the most valuable projects a worker can undertake is the development of a neighborhood youth council. Which one of the following is an ESSENTIAL factor in organizing such a council?   19._____

    A. The rules for membership should be those set forth by the youth services agency.
    B. The youths themselves should develop the purposes and general framework of the council.
    C. A police youth worker should be a key member of the adult advisory committee.
    D. Everyone in the neighborhood between the ages of 10 and 20 should be represented.

20. The one of the following which a worker should NOT encourage as an appropriate project for a neighborhood youth council is   20._____

    A. organizing a neighborhood block party
    B. planning an area clean-up or recycling campaign
    C. arranging an educational program on drug abuse among youth
    D. organizing a school strike and occupying the building

21. Some community workers in disadvantaged neighborhoods have taken on the role of   21.____
activist in working with local people.
Of the following, a worker who takes the position of *activist* would be MOST likely to

    A. encourage youth to engage in street riots as a form of protest
    B. insist that adolescent groups be given decision-making power in most areas
    C. play a direct role in promoting such actions as rent withholding, boycotts, or non-violent public demonstrations
    D. prepare proposals for increased government grants for youth services

22. Assume that there has been an incident in a poor socio-economic area in which several   22.____
youths were hurt in a *shoot-out*. A worker assigned to the area is approached by a
reporter from a newspaper, who asks him to identify the gangs involved.
The APPROPRIATE action for the worker to take would be to

    A. advise the reporter to contact his agency's public relations office
    B. talk to the reporter about the incident, but omit names of gangs
    C. give the reporter any facts he has
    D. tell the reporter that, in order to be able to work with gangs, he cannot become involved with the press

23. Assume that a worker who is planning to escort a 17-year-old youth in his group to court   23.____
is asked to testify in the youth's behalf by the youth's attorney.
The MOST advisable course of action for the worker to take would be to

    A. testify in order to help the youth
    B. consult his supervisor in order to arrive at a decision about testifying
    C. refuse to testify
    D. refuse to testify unless he can get permission from the youth's parents

24. A worker is approached by some members of a group called *Latin Lads,* who tell him that   24.____
they are now a social club and would like him to help them incorporate the club in order
to get a charter.
The worker should FIRST

    A. tell the group that this is not his job function
    B. contact a lawyer to help the group
    C. attempt to convince members to get responsible adults in the community involved in helping them get a charter
    D. discuss the process of getting a charter with the group and offer his name as a responsible adult

25. The community assistance function of a youth services agency is CORRECTLY   25.____
described as follows:

    A. Screening applications of community groups for federal grants to run summer youth programs
    B. Providing technical assistance to existing youth-serving organizations and helping communities to develop the additional resources needed to solve the most critical youth problems
    C. Mediating problems of jurisdiction among public and private community organizations serving youth
    D. Improving liaison between the police, the courts, and public and private community organizations serving youth, regarding juvenile offenders

KEY (CORRECT ANSWERS)

1.	A		11.	A
2.	A		12.	A
3.	A		13.	B
4.	C		14.	D
5.	B		15.	C
6.	B		16.	D
7.	B		17.	A
8.	C		18.	D
9.	A		19.	B
10.	C		20.	D

21.	C
22.	A
23.	B
24.	C
25.	B

———

TEST 2

DIRECTIONS: Each question or incomplete statement is followed by several suggested answers or completions. Select the one that BEST answers the question or completes the statement. *PRINT THE LETTER OF THE CORRECT ANSWER IN THE SPACE AT THE RIGHT.*

Questions 1-5.

DIRECTIONS: Questions 1 through 5 are to be answered SOLELY on the basis of the following paragraph.

There are several different schools of thought about the causes of juvenile delinquency. According to the "cultural-transmission" school of thought, delinquency is neither inborn nor developed independently. Children learn to become delinquents as members of groups in which delinquent conduct is already established and "the thing to do." This school maintains that a child need not be different from other children or have any problems or defects of personality or intelligence in order to become a delinquent. On the other hand, the "psychogenic" school views delinquency as a method of coping with some underlying problem of adjustment. This school also holds that the tendency to become delinquent is not inherited. The delinquent, however, has frustrations, deprivations, insecurities, anxieties, guilt feelings or mental conflicts which differ in kind or degree from those of non-delinquent children. Delinquency is thought of as a symptom of the underlying problem of adjustment in the same way as a fever is a symptom of an underlying infection. According to this school, if other children exhibit the same behavior, it is because they have independently found a similar solution to their problems.

1. Of the following, the MOST suitable title for the foregoing paragraph would be   1.____

    A.   Problems in the Scientific Study of Juvenile Delinquency
    B.   The Effect of Disturbed Family Situations
    C.   Two Theories of Juvenile Delinquency
    D.   Solutions to a Major Social Problem

2. According to the paragraph, the *cultural-transmission* school of thought holds that there   2.____
    is a definite relationship between juvenile delinquency and the youths'

    A.   intelligence   B.   psychological problems
    C.   family problems   D.   choice of friends

3. According to the paragraph, of the following, both schools of thought reject as a cause of   3.____
    juvenile delinquency the factor of

    A.   guilt feelings   B.   inherited traits
    C.   repeated frustration   D.   extreme insecurities

4. On the basis of the paragraph, which of the following statements is CORRECT?   4.____
    The

    A.   *cultural-transmission* school of thought maintains that a child independently develops delinquent behavior as a solution to his problems
    B.   *psychogenic* school of thought holds that children become delinquents because it is

    C.   *cultural-transmission* school of thought maintains that delinquency is the visible symptom of an underlying personality problem

    D.   *psychogenic* school of thought holds that delinquents have mental conflicts that differ in kind or degree from non-delinquents

5.   The author's attitude toward these schools of thought is that he   5._____

    A.   describes them objectively without indicating partiality to either school of thought

    B.   favors the *cultural-transmission* school of thought

    C.   favors the *psychogenic* school of thought

    D.   suggests that he thinks both schools of thought are incorrect

Questions 6-10.

DIRECTIONS: Questions 6 through 10 are to be answered SOLELY on the basis of the following paragraph.

    When a young boy or girl is released from one of the various facilities operated by the Division for youth, supportive services to help the youth face community, group, and family pressures are needed as much as, if not more than, at any other time. These services are the responsibility of two units of the Division for Youth, the Aftercare Unit, which serves youths discharged from the urban homes, camps, and START Centers, and the Community Service Bureaus, which serve youths released from the division's school and center programs. To assure that supportive services for released youths are easily identifiable and accessible, the division has developed the "store-front" services center, located in the heart of those areas to which many of the youngsters are returning. The storefront concept and structure is able to coordinate more closely services to the particular needs and situation of the youths and to draw on the feeling of community participation and achievement by persuading the community to join in helping them.

6.   Of the following, the BEST description of the storefront services center's relationship to neighborhood residents is that it   6._____

    A.   actively encourages their participation

    B.   accepts their help when offered

    C.   asks neighborhood residents to develop rehabilitation programs

    D.   limits participation to qualified neighborhood professional youth workers

7.   On the basis of the paragraph, which of the following statements is CORRECT?   7._____

    A.   Supportive services are not needed as much after a youth is released from a facility as during his stay.

    B.   Storefront services centers are located near the facilities operated by the Division for Youth.

    C.   The Community Service Bureaus serve youths released from urban homes.

    D.   Youths are given supportive services in their communities after release from facilities operated by the Division for Youth.

8. Of the following, the MOST suitable title for the foregoing paragraph would be   8.____

    A. Problems of Youths Returning to Society
    B. Community, Group, and Family Pressures on Released Youths
    C. Neighborhood Supportive Services for Released Youths
    D. A Survey of Facilities Operated by the Division for Youth

9. Which of the following characteristics of the storefront services is mentioned in the para-   9.____
graph?

    A. Cost   B. Availability
    C. Size   D. Complexity

10. On the basis of the paragraph, which of the following statements about the Aftercare Unit   10.____
is INCORRECT?
It

    A. is a part of the Division for Youth
    B. serves youths released from school programs
    C. is similar in function to the Community Service Bureaus
    D. was partly responsible for the development of storefront centers

Questions 11-20.

DIRECTIONS: In Questions 11 through 20, choose the lettered word or expression which is closest to the meaning of the first word or expression, *as used most frequently by street-oriented youth and members of youth gangs.* Do not try to give the usually accepted or dictionary definition of the word or expression.

11. copping   11.____

    A. stealing   B. lying
    C. squealing   D. harassing policemen

12. a geese   12.____

    A. stool pigeon   B. pulling a robbery
    C. lady pusher   D. free trip

13. jive stud   13.____

    A. lying braggart   B. wealthy drug pusher
    C. youth on probation   D. male prostitute with soul

14. turkey   14.____

    A. person easily manipulated by a gang member
    B. person who has been mugged
    C. discarded weapon
    D. beat-up car

15. a Jones   15.____

    A. a need for a fix   B. an alias
    C. a drug pusher   D. a fight for status

16. copping a plea   16.____

    A. testifying in court
    B. making up an excuse
    C. admitting guilt as originally charged
    D. asking a policeman for a favor

17. cold turkey   17.____

    A. giving up drugs
    B. kicking drugs without medication
    C. concealing a body
    D. keeping cool

18. dolls   18.____

    A. homosexuals   B. policewomen
    C. LSD   D. amphetamines

19. fair one   19.____

    A. heroin of good quality
    B. likeable white man
    C. fight between individual gang members
    D. rumble between two equal gangs

20. piece   20.____

    A. portion   B. loot   C. gun   D. pot

21. A good resource for a youth or adult who wants help in finding employment or obtaining   21.____
job training is the

    A. neighborhood manpower service center
    B. equal employment opportunity commission
    C. federation employment and guidance service
    D. economic development administration

22. It would be APPROPRIATE for a worker to refer a youth who is interested in vocational   22.____
training in such fields as keypunch operation, business machine repair, or food services
to the organization called

    A. Opportunities Industrialization Center
    B. Job Corps
    C. DSW Training Institute
    D. College for Human Services

23. Which of the following is a large group of business, religious, and educational institutions,   23.____
labor unions, and community organizations which have united in order to find solutions to
the problems of poverty and urban decay?

    A. New York Urban Coalition, Inc.
    B. Massive Neighborhood Economic Development, Inc.
    C. Council Against Poverty
    D. Interfaith Citywide Coordinating Committee Against Poverty

24. Which one of the following institutions for the care of adolescent boys is under the
    Department of Social Services?

    A. Jennings Hall
    B. New Hampton School for Boys
    C. Lincoln Hall
    D. Stuyvesant Residence Club

24.____

25. The Metropolitan Applied Research Center, Inc. is CORRECTLY described as a

    A. national organization which aims to improve living conditions of lower-income
urban residents through research, analysis, strategy development, and intervention
in areas such as economic opportunity, education, housing, health and welfare services, and consumer protection
    B. city agency which provides individual and group psychotherapy for patients of all
ages, races, and creeds and information and education in healthy emotional living
through interaction with all segments of the community
    C. branch of Metropolitan Hospital which includes guidance services for children and
adolescents and drug addiction, mental hygiene, and psychiatric walk-in clinics
    D. central city organization which fosters joint planning and participation of govern-
mental and voluntary social welfare organizations in research in the field of human
services

25.____

KEY (CORRECT ANSWERS)

1. C		11. A	
2. D		12. B	
3. B		13. A	
4. D		14. A	
5. A		15. A	
6. A		16. B	
7. D		17. B	
8. C		18. D	
9. B		19. C	
10. B		20. C	

21. A
22. A
23. A
24. A
25. A

EXAMINATION SECTION
TEST 1

DIRECTIONS: Each question or incomplete statement is followed by several suggested answers or completions. Select the one that BEST answers the question or completes the statement. *PRINT THE LETTER OF THE CORRECT ANSWER IN THE SPACE AT THE RIGHT.*

1. The MOST appropriate of the following actions for the worker to take in order to establish contact with street-oriented youths in a new neighborhood would be to   1.____

    A.   invite neighborhood teenagers and young adults to a party at the center
    B.   get a reputation for himself in the neighborhood by physically challenging an aggressive gang leader
    C.   visit the youths' hangouts, preferably in the company of a worker already known to them
    D.   post notices at the youths' hangouts, inviting them to come in and talk with him at the center

2. Of the following, the BEST statement of what the worker's aim should be during his first contacts with his assigned group is to   2.____

    A.   observe and study the group, and let them know his role
    B.   get a quick picture of their delinquent activities
    C.   convince the youths to meet in the youth center rather than on the streets
    D.   gain their respect as a person who represents authority

3. A worker is MOST likely to establish a constructive relationship with a group of street-oriented youths by   3.____

    A.   limiting activities to the interests and desires of the youths
    B.   setting limits and insisting that the youths accept responsibility for their behavior
    C.   accepting all available assistance from other agencies
    D.   socializing with the youths and trying to gain acceptance as a peer

4. It is essential that a relationship of trust and confidence be gradually established between the worker and his assigned group.
The one of the following which would NOT be a suitable method of developing such a relationship would be for the worker to   4.____

    A.   visit the homes of youth
    B.   play pool or participate in other recreational activities with them
    C.   be a *good listener*, giving advice when appropriate
    D.   try to gain acceptance as a group member

5. In promoting sports activities for street-oriented youth, it is ESSENTIAL for the worker to   5.____

    A.   play down the element of intense competition and keep activities low-keyed
    B.   stress competitive sports between gangs
    C.   arrange to award prizes to the winning teams
    D.   emphasize individual rather than team sports

6. Assume that a worker encounters a group of hostile youths for the first time in the basement of an abandoned building. The youths challenge him and claim that he is *a cop.* Of the following, the APPROPRIATE action for the worker to take would be to

    A. identify himself as a worker for the youth services agency and explain his role
    B. get out of the area as quickly as possible
    C. ignore the challenge and try to laught if off as a bad joke
    D. tell them that he is not a cop, but that they are in danger of getting into trouble with the police

6.____

7. If a worker should learn that a member of his group has been arrested by the police, it would usually be ADVISABLE for the worker to

    A. find a lawyer and encourage the group to raise money for legal fees
    B. help the youth get available legal assistance, and continue to counsel him and his family whenever appropriate
    C. discuss the boy's arrest with the other gang members as an example of what happens as a result of criminal activity
    D. become uninvolved and develop an objective and detached attitude toward the case

7.____

8. A worker is threatened with attack by a member of a youth ganc he is working with. Of the following, the step for the worker to take FIRST would be to

    A. get away fast before other gang members join in the attack
    B. face down the threat, overpowering the youth by surprise if necessary
    C. try to assess the situation and determine the seriousness of the threat
    D. remain calm and ignore the threat

8.____

9. Several youth gang members have pushed an abandoned car into the middle of the street and are smashing it with crowbars and hammers. When a worker asks them to stop, they say: *It's junk anyway. Why make such a stink?*
It would be APPROPRIATE for the worker to

    A. agree with them and let them go ahead and express their aggressive feelings
    B. urge them to stop, and try to convince them that they are making the neighborhood worse by wrecking the car
    C. call a wrecking company and have the car towed away
    D. ignore the entire matter

9.____

10. Assume that a worker has planned to take six gang members on a trip in his station wagon. At the last minute, four more boys want to go. Although there is room for only six in the station wagon, the boys urge him to cram everybody in.
It would be ADVISABLE for the worker to

    A. try to cram all the boys into the station wagon
    B. take only the original six boys, pointing out that overloading the car might cause an accident
    C. have the boys draw lots and take the six who win
    D. call off the trip, since it has become the cause of a dispute

10.____

11. A worker attends a rap session at the meeting place of his group. Some of the members   11.____
boast about how often they have been heavily drunk.
Of the following, it would be MOST advisable for the worker to

    A. ignore the comments as being youthful boasting
    B. tell them that if he ever sees them drinking, he will confiscate the liquor
    C. laugh and say that he sometimes gets drunk too
    D. point out that people often lose their cool and get into serious trouble while drunk

12. If a worker should become aware of widespread drug use by youths in his group, of the   12.____
following, it would be MOST advisable to

    A. discuss the dangers of drug abuse with them, and refer those with a serious drug
       problem to an appropriate treatment agency
    B. try to change their attitudes towards drugs by giving them reading material such as
       fliers and other literature about drug abuse
    C. let them know that heroin is considered to be the real threat and that pills and mar-
       ijuana are considered to be less dangerous
    D. disregard this knowledge until it becomes necessary to handle a serious problem
       of an individual youth

13. Assume that a worker has determined for a fact that a member of his group is using hard   13.____
drugs.
The FIRST step for the worker to take would be to

    A. confront the youth and discuss the problem with him
    B. refer the youth to the state narcotics control commission
    C. discuss the problem with his supervisor
    D. meet with the youth's parents

14. A worker discovers that youth groups in his neighborhood are being contacted by an out-   14.____
side pusher of hard drugs. Of the following, the MOST advisable step for him to take
would be to

    A. trail the pusher back to his source of supply, notify the police, and try to arrange a
       large-scale arrest of all those involved
    B. try to get evidence by photographing the pusher in the act of distributing drugs, or
       making tape recordings of meetings with the youths
    C. instruct the youth group leaders to notify the police, since a youth worker is not
       qualified to participate in handling such a situation
    D. meet with the leaders of the groups involved, help them understand the danger to
       their members, and urge them to keep the neighborhood clean

15. A worker has definite evidence that a member of a neighborhood gang has set several   15.____
fires in tenements, one of which resulted in a fatality.
Of the following, the FIRST step to take would be to

    A. give this information to the police
    B. talk to the youth privately and urge him to get psychiatric treatment
    C. watch him and try to catch him in the act of setting a fire
    D. talk to the youth's parents and tell them that the police will be informed if the boy
       sets another fire

16. A worker has reliable information about the time and place of an impending rumble between his assigned group and members of another gang. The gangs are armed, and on their way to the rumble.
Of the following, the action to take FIRST would be to

    A. call his supervisor
    B. inform the police
    C. try to convince his group not to fight the others
    D. inform the youths' families

16.____

17. Assume that a worker is interviewing a boy in his assigned group in order to help him find a job.
At the beginning of the interview, the worker should

    A. suggest a possible job for the youth
    B. refer the youth to an employment agency
    C. discuss the youth's work history and skills with him
    D. refer the youth to the manpower and career development agency

17.____

18. An important service provided by the youth services agency is the promotion of recreational activities for street-oriented youth.
Of the following, the MOST suitable type of recreation program would be

    A. arranging a weekly rock-and-roll dance at a neighborhood center situated on the borderline between the turfs of rival gangs
    B. assisting the youths with sports programs, helping them to get facilities, coaching, setting up a schedule, etc.
    C. teaching individual youths hobbies such as jewelry-making or tie-dying
    D. planning a fundraising drive to enable youths to take a plane trip to some vacation area

18.____

19. A worker is helping a youth group in a high-tension neighborhood to arrange a dance.
He should advise the group to

    A. publicize the dance widely, in and out of the neighborhood, in order to bring in a big crowd
    B. set up a *gate committee* to keep out outsiders by force, if necessary
    C. restrict admission to gang members and their friends or neighborhood youth by invitation only
    D. make it a big money-raising affair, so that the gang can build a *rep*

19.____

20. Assume that a worker has been informed by a group member that Johnny, a member of a group called the *Black Aces,* is *packing* to *go down* on the Bishop.
The FIRST step that the worker should take is to

    A. speak to the group and ask them not to follow Johnny
    B. encourage Johnny to give him his weapon
    C. inform the police that Johnny is *packing*
    D. tell the group member that he should not *rat* on Johnny

20.____

21. Assume that a worker has gone on a bus ride to a park with 50 community youths, who had been told beforehand that they could not bring liquor of any kind with them. However, when the bus reaches the park, he discovers that they have brought a considerable amount of wine.
    Which of the following courses of action should the worker take?   21.____

    A. Alert the park police about the contraband
    B. Discuss the situation with the youths in order to make a group decision
    C. Destroy all the bottles of wine
    D. Instruct the youths to stay on the bus and order the driver to return to the neighborhood

22. If a worker should learn that a youth in his group has committed an armed robbery, it is his obligation to   22.____

    A. immediately inform his supervisor, who will see that the police are informed
    B. record the information in his weekly report to his supervisor
    C. refer the youth to the youth counsel bureau
    D. assure the youth that he will not report him to the police if he does not turn himself in

23. Assume that a worker has definite evidence that one of his group members is *pushing* hard drugs.
    Which of the following steps should he take IMMEDIATELY?   23.____

    A. Inform his supervisor, who will then be responsible for notifying the police
    B. Tell the policeman on the beat about the problem
    C. Confront the youth and tell him that the police will be informed
    D. Keep this information to himself in order to safeguard confidentiality

24. Assume that a worker finds a youth in his group *OD* in the group meeting room.
    Of the following, the step to take FIRST would be to   24.____

    A. call the youth's parents
    B. notify the police to summon an ambulance
    C. determine the quantity of drugs taken by the youth
    D. give first aid to the youth

25. Assume that a recently appointed worker arrives at a basement club for a meeting with his group and finds that the boys are smoking pot.
    At this point, it would be ADVISABLE for the worker to   25.____

    A. leave the premises
    B. join the group
    C. warn the boys about the dangers of smoking pot
    D. inform the police

_____

KEY (CORRECT ANSWERS)

1.	C		11.	D
2.	A		12.	A
3.	B		13.	A
4.	D		14.	D
5.	A		15.	A
6.	A		16.	B
7.	B		17.	C
8.	C		18.	B
9.	B		19.	C
10.	B		20.	C

21. D
22. A
23. A
24. B
25. A

———

TEST 2

Questions 1-5.

DIRECTIONS: Questions 1 through 5 relate to the problems of Bill, Robert, and Stan, three members of a youth gang who have dropped out of school and have asked the worker to help them find jobs.

1. Assume that the worker learns that Bill is unable to get a job through employment agencies because he has a record of several arrests.
   It would be DESIRABLE for the worker to

   A. tell Bill that he is not qualified to help him under such circumstances
   B. tell Bill that the only solution is to join the Army in order to straighten his record out
   C. recommend that Bill see a caseworker for vocational counseling
   D. encourage one of the neighborhood businessmen to hire Bill

1.____

2. Suppose that Bill manages to get a job as a delivery boy, but gets bored after a few weeks and quits.
   At this point, it would be BEST for the worker, to

   A. devote less attention to Bill, since he has been irresponsible
   B. send Bill to the state employment service
   C. help Bill to get employment counseling
   D. discuss the situation with Bill and try to get him to understand his problems

2.____

3. Robert is unable to get a job because he has no vocational skills and cannot read or write. Nevertheless, he is not willing to go back to school or into an organized remedial education program.
   Of the following, the MOST appropriate step for the worker to take would be to

   A. tell Robert that remedial education is the only choice he has, and if he will not do this he can no longer be helped
   B. try to arrange one-to-one tutoring for Robert through a special agency or with a volunteer youth or adult
   C. reassure Robert by telling him that he does not need to learn to read or write to be a laborer
   D. meet with Robert an hour or two every day, to teach him the basic reading and writing skills

3.____

4. Stan indicates that he realizes he would be better off finishing high school before going to work full-time. However, his family cannot support him fully as a student. Of the following, it would be MOST appropriate for the worker to

   A. meet with the high school guidance counselor in order to discuss Stan's problem
   B. tell Stan that he will arrange a loan for him from the neighborhood bank
   C. arrange to go with Stan for a meeting with the school guidance counselor to help him explain his problem
   D. suggest that Stan work for a while in order to save enough money to go back to school

4.____

5. Assume that all three youths have developed an emotional dependence on the worker, thinking of him as a father. The worker would be MOST helpful if he

    A. continues to give the boys emotional support and guidance, gradually helping them to become more independent
    B. keeps the youths as dependent as possible, until they are fully grown up
    C. keeps this kind of relationship from developing, because the youths' real fathers may be jealous
    D. has them transferred to another worker, in order to break up this dependency

5.____

Questions 6-7.

DIRECTIONS: Questions 6 and 7 relate to the problems of a worker who is working with a group of youths between 18 and 20 years of age.

6. Assume that a worker learns that Michael, one of the youths he has been working with, has been having relations with a 16-year-old girl, Connie, who is now pregnant. The worker's FIRST step should be to

    A. talk with Michael to find out the facts
    B. go to see Connie's mother to tell her the situation
    C. report Michael to the police, because Connie is only 16
    D. suggest to Michael that he send money to Connie each week

6.____

7. Michael tells the worker that, while he might be the father of Connie's baby, he is not sure because she has had relations with several other boys. Other gang members confirm this. Michael says that he does not love Connie. It would be ADVISABLE for the worker to

    A. agree with Michael that he has no responsibility for Connie
    B. encourage Michael to marry Connie for the child's sake
    C. speak to Connie and encourage her to go to a family service agency
    D. urge Connie to have an abortion

7.____

8. An adult in the community has told a worker that he has heard that two members of his group have *ripped off* an elderly lady in the housing project.
Of the following, the BEST action for the worker to take would be to

    A. conceal from the youths the fact that he has been told about this incident
    B. immediately notify the police about the incident
    C. discuss the incident with the youths who have been accused in order to get more information
    D. discuss the incident with the youths' parents

8.____

9. When a youth comes into the neighborhood office and asks for help in finding a job, the worker's FIRST consideration should be whether

    A. the youth has the capacity for skills training
    B. the need for a job is the youth's real problem
    C. the youth can hold a job
    D. a job for this youth is available immediately

9.____

10. A worker checks into the field and learns that his group members are picketing the local school and are threatening to use violence to keep the school closed. The police are already at the scene.
At this point, it would be ADVISABLE for the worker to

    10.____

    A.   join the picket line in order to keep an eye on his group members
    B.   contact the office and discuss the situation with his supervisor
    C.   stay at the school and wait for an opportune moment to confront the group
    D.   identify himself to the police and try to help them control the group

11. In an attempt to get it out of his possession, a group member tries to give a handgun to a worker whom he meets on the street.
Of the following, the MOST advisable action for the worker to take would be to

    11.____

    A.   refuse to accept the gun and tell the youth that he is going to inform the police
    B.   accept the gun and get rid of it as soon as possible
    C.   accept the gun and turn it over to the police
    D.   refuse to accept the gun and tell the youth to get rid of it

12. The one of the following which would be the BEST technique for a worker to use in order to prevent a violent conflict between rival youth groups in different neighborhoods is to

    12.____

    A.   try to arrange a meeting of both gangs in a neutral spot, so that they can talk it over and make peace
    B.   suggest that the *warlords* of both gangs settle the dispute by fighting it out in a nearby gym
    C.   contact the worker serving with the other group in order to share information about the issues and work out a plan to prevent the conflict
    D.   arrange to take the members of your group on a trip in the hope that the trouble will be over when you return

13. If a worker is told that a youth in his assigned group has been expelled from school, the BEST way to approach the problem FIRST would be to

    13.____

    A.   discuss this information with the youth
    B.   contact the youth's parents
    C.   meet with the school guidance counselor
    D.   contact the principal and find out why he was expelled

14. The BEST of the following methods for the worker to use in order to gain the cooperation and confidence of youths in his group is to

    14.____

    A.   promise only what he is reasonably sure he can deliver, in terms of special help
    B.   let them know that he will be able to get them out of trouble with the police
    C.   treat them to drinks or cigarettes, and lend them money in emergencies
    D.   make extensive promises about the special facilities and services he can get for them

15. When faced with illegal activity on the part of gang members, some workers say: *It is not my job to turn them in. I warn them that if they continue with this behavior, they are likely to be arrested, but I will never inform the police myself.*
    This attitude on the part of workers toward illegal activity by gang members is

    A. *acceptable,* mainly because gang members are likely to resist any attempt to control them
    B. *unacceptable,* mainly because the boys may think he can be manipulated
    C. *acceptable,* mainly because it will help gang members recognize the reality of their conflict with society
    D. *unacceptable,* mainly because the boys may resent his interference

15.____

16. After a worker has gained the acceptance of the youths in his group, he should devote his efforts to accomplishing certain key objectives.
    The one of the following which would NOT be an appropriate key objective in working with the group is to

    A. attempt to control anti-social activities by the group
    B. help rehabilitate youths who exhibit anti-social behavior
    C. develop opportunities for education, employment, and constructive social activities
    D. encourage youths to drift away in order to break up the group

16.____

17. Assume that a worker is told by a youth in his assigned group that five gang members are having a *line-up* on an adolescent girl in their basement clubroom.
    The worker's FIRST step should be to

    A. report the incident to the police
    B. have the youth accompany him to the clubroom
    C. inform the girl's parents
    D. call a meeting of the gang group to discuss their criminal behavior

17.____

18. Which of the following is a key factor in the development of a constructive relationship between a worker and his group of street-oriented youth?
    The

    A. group members identify with the worker
    B. worker identifies with the members of his group
    C. group members feel that the worker accepts them as they are, with all their strengths and weaknesses
    D. worker regularly participates in the activities of the group

18.____

19. Assume that a group of youths, with the help of a worker, have just made satisfactory arrangements for the use of a gymnasium in a community center. On the way out of the center, one of the boys picks up a rock and indicates that he is going to throw it through a window.
    The one of the following approaches which would probably be MOST effective is for the worker to tell the boy that he

    A. would be a poor sport to damage the property so soon after being given permission to use the center's facilities
    B. will give their group a bad reputation if it is discovered that they caused damage so soon after being given access to the gymnasium
    C. would be foolish to give vent to his hostility by breaking a window
    D. will cause the boys to lose the use of the gymnasium if he breaks the window

19.____

20. When a worker is given a new assignment in an unfamiliar neighborhood, the MOST 20.____
    important step for him to take FIRST would be to

    A. meet with local school principals and have them outline the major youth problems
       in the community
    B. make an informal survey of the community in order to define the scope of youth
       problems and needs
    C. contact the local police precinct and ask them to identify problem youth and youth
       groups in the community
    D. walk the streets, primarily in order to determine criminal activities involving youth

21. Suppose that a worker, during his first interview with a member of his group, finds that 21.____
    the youth is becoming antagonistic to him for no apparent reason.
    Of the following, it would be BEST for the worker to

    A. convince the youth that there is no basis for his antagonism before continuing the
       interview
    B. terminate the interview and ask the youth to come back when he feels friendlier
    C. insist that the youth explain why he feels antagonistic to him before continuing the
       interview
    D. continue the interview in an understanding manner, without showing signs of dis-
       approval

22. As a means of improving neighborhood control over juvenile delinquent activity, of the fol- 22.____
    lowing, it would be MOST useful for the worker to

    A. make a survey in order to become knowledgeable about criminal adult activities in
       the neighborhood
    B. develop constructive relationships with key neighborhood residents who may coop-
       erate with him in helping delinquent youth
    C. establish himself as an authority figure in order to strengthen the control structure
       established by the police
    D. try to change the leadership structure of neighborhood gang groups in order to
       take control away from delinquent gang leaders

23. Assume that a local tavern owner who runs a crap game in his back room makes an offer 23.____
    to a worker to provide food and transportation for an outing being planned for his gang
    group.
    It would be ADVISABLE for the worker to

    A. refuse the offer at once
    B. accept the tavern owner's help
    C. refuse the offer and report the tavern owner's illegal activities to the police
    D. ask his supervisor whether he should accept the tavern owner's help

24. Assume that a group of 40 businessmen and property-owners in a disadvantaged neighborhood are holding a meeting to discuss the problem of vandalism by local youth gang members. Three of the businessmen are hostile and uncooperative, making it difficult for the others to consider the problem in a rational manner.
Which of the following would be MOST likely to intensify such hostility and uncooperative behavior?

    A. Appointing a committee which includes the disgruntled members to look into various aspects of the problem
    B. Insisting upon the will of the majority
    C. Having the group as a whole discuss the reasons for the hostility
    D. Making concessions to the hostile members

24.____

25. Assume that the principal of the local junior high school has been complaining about gang activities in and around the school, and that a worker has been assigned to look into the situation.
The MOST appropriate action for the worker to take FIRST is to

    A. meet with the patrolman on the beat to discuss the situation
    B. ask the principal to assemble the youths in order to question them about their activities
    C. visit the school in order to observe any anti-social activities and to assess the problem
    D. advise the principal to report the gang members to the local police precinct

25.____

KEY (CORRECT ANSWERS)

1.	D		11.	A
2.	D		12.	C
3.	B		13.	A
4.	C		14.	A
5.	A		15.	B
6.	A		16.	D
7.	C		17.	B
8.	C		18.	C
9.	B		19.	D
10.	B		20.	B

21.	D
22.	B
23.	A
24.	B
25.	C

READING COMPREHENSION
UNDERSTANDING AND INTERPRETING WRITTEN MATERIAL
EXAMINATION SECTION
TEST 1

DIRECTIONS: Each question or incomplete statement is followed by several suggested answers or completions. Select the one that BEST answers the question or completes the statement. *PRINT THE LETTER OF THE CORRECT ANSWER IN THE SPACE AT THE RIGHT.*

Questions 1-5.

DIRECTIONS: Questions 1 through 5 are to be answered SOLELY on the basis of the following paragraph.

There are several different schools of thought about the causes of juvenile delinquency. According to the *cultural-transmission* school of thought, delinquency is neither inborn nor developed independently. Children learn to become delinquents as members of groups in which delinquent conduct is already established and *the thing to do.* This school maintains that a child need not be different from other children or have any problems or defects of personality or intelligence in order to become a delinquent. On the other hand, the *psychogenic* school views delinquency as a method of coping with some underlying problem of adjustment. This school also holds that the tendency to become delinquent is not inherited. The delinquent, however, has frustrations, deprivations, insecurities, anxieties, guilt feelings, or mental conflicts which differ in kind or degree from those of non-delinquent children. Delinquency is thought of as a symptom of the underlying problem of adjustment in the same way as a fever is a symptom of an underlying infection. According to this school, if other children exhibit the same behavior, it is because they have independently found a similar solution to their problems.

1.   Of the following, the MOST suitable title for the above paragraph would be   1.____

    A.   PROBLEMS IN THE SCIENTIFIC STUDY OF JUVENILE DELINQUENCY
    B.   THE EFFECT OF DISTURBED FAMILY SITUATION
    C.   TWO THEORIES OF JUVENILE DELINQUENCY
    D.   SOLUTIONS TO A MAJOR SOCIAL PROBLEM

2.   According to the above paragraph, the *cultural-transmission* school of thought holds that   2.____
there is a definite relationship between juvenile delinquency and the youths'

    A.   intelligence   B.   psychological problems
    C.   family problems   D.   choice of friends

3.   According to the above paragraph, of the following, both schools of thought reject as a   3.____
cause of juvenile delinquency the factor of

    A.   guilt feelings   B.   inherited traits
    C.   repeated frustration   D.   extreme insecurities

4. On the basis of the above paragraph, which of the following statements is CORRECT? 4.____

    A. The *cultural-transmission* school of thought maintains that a child independently develops delinquent behavior as a solution to his problems.
    B. The *psychogenic* school of thought holds that children become delinquents because it is *the thing to do.*
    C. The *cultural-transmission* school of thought maintains that delinquency is the visible symptom of an underlying personality problem.
    D. The *psychogenic* school of thought holds that delinquents have mental conflicts that differ in kind or degree from non-delinquents.

5. The author's attitude toward these schools of thought is that he 5.____

    A. describes them objectively without indicating partiality to either school of thought
    B. favors the *cultural-transmission* school of thought
    C. favors the *psychogenic* school of thought
    D. suggests that he thinks both schools of thought are incorrect

Questions 6-7.

DIRECTIONS: Questions 6 and 7 are to be answered SOLELY on the basis of the following paragraph.

Behavior that seems strange to adults often is motivated by the child's desire to please his peers or to gain their attention. His feelings when ridiculed by his peers may range from grief to rage. It is difficult for the child to express such feelings and the reasons for them to adults for to do so he must admit to himself the bitter fact that persons whose friendship he wants really do not like him. Instead of directly expressing his feelings, he may reveal them through symptoms such as fault-finding, fighting back, and complaining. As a result, adults may not realize that when he is telling them how much he dislikes certain children, he may really be expressing how much he would like to be liked by these same children, or how deeply he feels contempt of himself.

6. This paragraph implies that a child's constant complaints about certain other children may be his way of expressing 6.____

    A. his desire to be accepted by them
    B. his dislike of the adults around him
    C. ridicule for those he does not like
    D. how many faults those other children have

7. According to the above paragraph, a child may find it difficult to express his grief at being rejected by his peer group because 7.____

    A. his rejection motivates him to behave strangely
    B. he knows that the adults around him would not understand his grief
    C. he may not be able to admit the fact of his rejection to himself
    D. his anger prevents him from expressing grief

Questions 8-9.

DIRECTIONS: Questions 8 and 9 are to be answered SOLELY on the basis of the following
paragraph.

A very small child has no concept of right or wrong. However, as soon as he is sufficiently
developed to be aware of forces outside himself, he will begin to see the advantage of behaving so as to win approval and avoid punishment. If the parents' standard of behavior is presented to the child in a consistent manner, the child will begin to incorporate that standard
within himself so that he feels the urge to do what his parents want him to do, whether they
are there or not. Furthermore, he will feel uncomfortable doing what he thinks is wrong even if
there is no probability of discovery and punishment. If the parents' standard of behavior is
NOT consistent, the child may grow up too confused to establish any ideal for himself. We
then have a youngster who truly does not know right from wrong. He is in danger of having no
firm standard of behavior, no conscience, and no feeling of guilt in defying the established
community pattern.

8.   The author of the above passage implies that a child whose parents do NOT present him   8._____
with a consistent standard of behavior

A.   will learn the difference between right and wrong when he is older
B.   may feel no guilt when committing delinquent acts
C.   will feel uncomfortable doing what he thinks is wrong
D.   is likely to establish his own ideal standards

9.   The above paragraph implies that when a child feels the urge to do what his parents want   9._____
him to do, even if they are not present, it means that the child

A.   sees the advantages of behaving so as to avoid punishment
B.   has no concept of right and wrong
C.   has begun to develop a conscience based on his parents' standard of behavior
D.   is afraid that his parents will find out if he misbehaves

Questions 10-13.

DIRECTIONS: Questions 10 through 13 are to be answered SOLELY on the basis of the information in the following passage.

NEW YORK CITY GANGS

City social work agencies and the police have been meeting at City Hall to coordinate
efforts to defuse the tensions among teenage groups that they fear could flare into warfare
once summer vacations begin. Police intelligence units, with the help of the District Attorneys'
offices, are gathering information to identify gangs and their territories. A list of 3,000 gang
members has already been assembled, and 110 gangs have been identified. Social workers
from various agencies like the Department of Social Services, Neighborhood Youth Corps,
and the Youth Board, are out every day developing liaison with groups of juveniles through
meetings at schools and recreation centers. Many street workers spend their days seeking to
ease the intergang hostility, tracing potentially incendiary rumors, and trying to channel willing
gang members into participation in established summer programs. The city's Youth Services
Agency plans to spend a million dollars for special summer programs in ten main city areas
where gang activity is most firmly entrenched. Five of the *gang neighborhoods* are clustered
in an area forming most of southeastern Bronx, and it is here that most of the 110 identified

gangs have formed. Special Youth Services programs will also be directed toward the Rock-away section of Queens, Chinatown, Washington Heights, and two neighborhoods in northern Staten Island noted for a lot of motorcycle gang activity. Some of these programs will emphasize sports and recreation, others vocational guidance or neighborhood improvement, but each program will be aimed at benefiting all youngsters in the area. Although none of the money will be spent specifically on gang members, the Youth Services Agency is consulting gang leaders, along with other teenagers, on the projects they would like developed in their area.

10. The above passage states that one of the steps taken by street workers in trying to defuse the tensions among teenage gangs is that of

    10._____

    A. conducting summer school sessions that will benefit all neighborhood youth
    B. monitoring neighborhood sports competitions between rival gangs
    C. developing liaison with community school boards and parent associations
    D. tracing rumors that could intensify intergang hostilities

11. Based on the information given in the above passage on gangs and New York City's gang members, it is CORRECT to state that

    11._____

    A. there are no teenage gangs located in Brooklyn
    B. most of the gangs identified by the Police are concentrated in one borough
    C. there is a total of 110 gangs in New York City
    D. only a small percentage of gangs in New York City is in Queens

12. According to the above passage, one IMPORTANT aspect of the program is that

    12._____

    A. youth gang leaders and other teenagers are involved in the planning
    B. money will be given directly to gang members for use on their projects
    C. only gang members will be allowed to participate in the programs
    D. the parents of gang members will act as youth leaders

13. Various city agencies are cooperating in the attempt to keep the city's youth *cool* during the summer school vacation period.
The above passage does NOT specifically indicate participation in this project by the

    13._____

    A. Police Department
    B. District Attorney's Office
    C. Board of Education
    D. Department of Social Services

Questions 14-16.

DIRECTIONS: Questions 14 through 16 are to be answered SOLELY on the basis of the following paragraph.

Drug abuse prevention efforts are only in their beginning stages. Far less is known about how to design programs that successfully counter the seductive effects which drugs have upon the young than about how to build clinics and programs to treat those who have become addicts. The latter can be done with enough dollars, managerial competence, and qualified personnel. The former depends upon such intangibles as community leadership, personal attitudes, and, in the final analysis, individual choices. Given this void in our society's understanding of what it is that makes us so vulnerable to addiction, government must build upon its growing experience to invest wisely in those efforts that offer positive alternatives to drug abuse.

14. The one of the following which is probably the BEST title for the above paragraph is   14.____

    A. THE YOUTHFUL DRUG ABUSER
    B. GOVERNMENT'S MANAGEMENT OF DRUG PROGRAMS
    C. A SCIENTIFIC ANALYSIS OF DRUG CURES
    D. THE DIFFICULTY OF DRUG ABUSE PREVENTION

15. According to the above paragraph, treating drug addicts as compared to preventing drug   15.____
addiction among the young is GENERALLY

    A. *easier,* mainly because there is more public interest in this method
    B. *harder,* mainly because qualified personnel are not readily available
    C. *easier,* mainly because there is more known about how to accomplish this objective
    D. *harder,* mainly because confirmed drug addicts do not give up the habit readily

16. According to the above paragraph, the role of government in dealing with the problem of   16.____
drug addiction and youth should be to

    A. build larger clinics and develop additional programs for treatment of offenders
    B. help attract youth to behavior which is more desirable than that provided by the drug culture
    C. provide the funds and personnel essential to successful enforcement programs
    D. establish centers for the study and analysis of those factors that make our citizens vulnerable to addiction

Questions 17-20.

DIRECTIONS: Questions 17 through 20 are to be answered SOLELY on the basis of the following paragraph.

    Many of our city's most troubled drug addicts are not being reached by the existing treatment programs. They either refuse to enter treatment voluntarily or have dropped out of these programs. A substantial number of the city's heroin addicts, including some of the most crime-prone, are unlikely to be reached by the mere expansion of existing treatment programs.

17. According to the above paragraph, the drug addicts who have dropped out of existing   17.____
programs

    A. are habitual criminals beyond hope of chance
    B. could be reached by expanding existing programs
    C. include the seriously disturbed
    D. had been compelled to enroll in such programs

18. According to the above paragraph, some drug addicts are not being aided by current   18.____
treatment efforts because those addicts

    A. are serving excessively long prison sentences
    B. are unwilling to become involved in programs
    C. have been accepted by therapeutic communities
    D. have lost confidence in the city's programs

19. As used in the above paragraph, the underlined word <u>prone</u> means MOST NEARLY   19.____

    A. angered   B. bold   C. exclusive   D. inclined

20. As used in the above paragraph, the underlined word <u>mere</u> means MOST NEARLY   20.____

    A. formal   B. simple   C. remote   D. prompt

Questions 21-23.

DIRECTIONS: Questions 21 through 23 are to be answered SOLELY on the basis of the following passage.

    A survey of the drinking behavior of 1,185 persons representing the adult population of Iowa in 2008 aged 21 years and older revealed that approximately 40 percent were abstainers. Of the nearly one million drinkers in the State, 47 percent were classed as light drinkers, 37 percent as moderate, and 16 percent as heavy drinkers. Twenty-two percent of the men drinkers were classed as heavy drinkers but only 8 percent of the women drinkers. The proportion of heavy drinkers increased with level of education among drinkers residing in the city - from 15 percent of the least educated to 22 percent of the most educated; but decreased among farm residents from 17 percent of the least educated to 4 percent of the most educated. Age differences in the extent of drinking were not pronounced. The age class of 36-45 had the lowest proportions of light drinkers, while the age class 61 and over had the lowest proportion of heavy drinkers.

21. According to the above passage, which one of the following statements concerning heavy drinking would be CORRECT?   21.____

    A. Experts are in sharp conflict regarding the reason for heavy drinking.
    B. The amount of heavy drinking in the city is directly proportional to the amount of education.
    C. The degree of heavy drinking is directly proportional to the age class of the drinkers.
    D. The degree of heavy drinking is inversely to the number of light drinkers.

22. Of the total drinking population in Iowa, how many were moderate drinkers?   22.____

    A. 370,000   B. 438   C. 370   D. 438,150

23. What percent of the men drinkers surveyed were NOT heavy drinkers?   23.____

    A. 60%   B. 84%
    C. 78%   D. Cannot be determined

Questions 24-25.

DIRECTIONS: Questions 24 and 25 are to be answered SOLELY on the basis of the following paragraph.

    A drug-user does not completely retreat from society. While a new user, he must begin participation in some group of old users in order to secure access to a steady supply of drugs. In the process, his readiness to engage in drug use, which stems from his personality and the social structure, is reinforced by new patterns of associations and values. The more the individual is caught in this web of associations, the more likely it is that he will persist in drug use, for he has become incorporated into a subculture that exerts control over his behavior. However, it is also true that the resulting tics among addicts are not as strong as those among participants in criminal and conflict subcultures. Addiction is in many ways an individualistic adaptation for the *kick* is essentially a private experience. The compelling need for the drug is also a divisive force for it leads to intense competition among addicts for money. Forces of this kind thus limit the relative cohesion which can develop among users.

24. According to the above paragraph, the MAIN reason why new drug users associate with old users is a   24.____

   A. fear of the police
   B. common hatred of society
   C. need to get drugs
   D. dislike of being alone

25. According to the above paragraph, which of the following statements is INCORRECT?   25.____

   A. Drug users encourage each other to continue taking drugs.
   B. Gangs that use drugs are more cohesive than other delinquent gangs.
   C. A youth's desire to use drugs stems from his personality as well as the social struc-
      ture.
   D. Addicts get no more of a *kick* from using drugs in a group than alone.

_____

KEY (CORRECT ANSWERS)

1.	C		11.	B
2.	D		12.	A
3.	B		13.	C
4.	D		14.	D
5.	A		15.	C
6.	A		16.	B
7.	C		17.	C
8.	B		18.	B
9.	C		19.	D
10.	D		20.	B

21.	B
22.	A
23.	C
24.	C
25.	B

_____

101

TEST 2

DIRECTIONS: Each question or incomplete statement is followed by several suggested answers or completions. Select the one that BEST answers the question or completes the statement. *PRINT THE LETTER OF THE CORRECT ANSWER IN THE SPACE AT THE RIGHT.*

Questions 1-5.

DIRECTIONS: Questions 1 through 5 are to be answered SOLELY on the basis of the following passage.

In an attempt to describe what is meant by a delinquent subculture, let us look at some delinquent activities. We usually assume that when people steal things, they steal because they want them to eat or wear or otherwise use them; or because they can sell them; or even –if we are given to a psychoanalytic turn of mind–because on some deep symbolic level the things stolen substitute or stand for something unconsciously desired but forbidden. However, most delinquent gang stealing has no such utilitarian motivation at all. Even where the value of the object stolen is itself a motivating consideration, the stolen sweets are often sweeter than those acquired by more legitimate and prosaic means. In homelier language, stealing *for the hell of it* and apart from considerations of gain and profit is a valued activity to which attaches glory, prowess, and profound satisfaction.

Similarly, many other delinquent activities are motivated mainly by an enjoyment in the distress of others and by a hostility toward non-gang peers as well as adults. Apart from the more dramatic manifestations in the form of gang wars, there is keen delight in terrorizing *good* children and in driving them from playgrounds and gyms for which the gang itself may have little use. The same spirit is evident in playing hooky and in misbehavior in school. The teacher and her rules are not merely to be evaded. They are to be flouted.

All this suggests that the delinquent subculture is not only a set of rules, a design for living which is different from or indifferent to or even in conflict with the norms of the *respectable* adult society. It actually takes its norms from the larger culture but turns them upside down. The delinquent's conduct is right, by the standards of his subculture, precisely BECAUSE it is wrong by the standards of the larger culture.

1.   Of the following, the MOST suitable title for the above passage is   1.____

   A.   DIFFERENT KINDS OF DELINQUENT SUBCULTURES
   B.   DELINQUENT HOSTILITY TOWARD NON-GANG PEERS
   C.   METHODS OF DELINQUENT STEALING
   D.   DELINQUENT STANDARDS AS REVEALED BY THEIR ACTIVITIES

2.   It may be inferred from the above passage that MOST delinquent stealing is motivated by a   2.____

   A.   need for food and clothing
   B.   need for money to buy drugs
   C.   desire for peer-approval
   D.   symbolic identification of the thing stolen with hidden desires

3. The passage IMPLIES that an important reason why delinquents play hooky and misbehave in school is that the teachers

   A. represent *respectable* society
   B. are boring
   C. have not taught them the values of the adult society
   D. are too demanding

3.____

4. In the above passage, the author's attitude toward delinquents is

   A. critical   B. objective
   C. overly sympathetic   D. confused

4.____

5. According to the above passage, which of the following statements is CORRECT?

   A. Delinquents derive no satisfaction from stealing.
   B. Delinquents are not hostile toward someone without a reason.
   C. The common motive of many delinquent activities is a desire to frustrate others.
   D. The delinquent subculture shares its standards with the *respectable* adult culture.

5.____

Questions 6-8.

DIRECTIONS: Questions 6 through 8 are to be answered SOLELY on the basis of the follow-
              ing paragraph.

A fundamental part of the youth worker's role is changing the interaction patterns which
already exist between the delinquent group and the representatives of key institutions in the
community; e.g., the policeman, teacher, social worker, employer, parent, and storekeeper.
This relationship, particularly its definitional character, is a two-way proposition. The offending
youth or group will usually respond by fulfilling this prophecy. In the same way, the delinquent
expects punishment or antagonistic treatment from officials and other representatives of middle class society. In turn, the adult concerned may act to fulfill the prophecy of the delinquent.
Stereotyped patterns of expectation, both of the delinquents and those in contact with them,
must be changed. The worker can be instrumental in changing these patterns.

6. Of the following, the MOST suitable title for the above paragraph is

   A. WAYS TO PREDICT JUVENILE DELINQUENCY
   B. THE YOUTH WORKER'S ROLE IN CREATING STEREOTYPES
   C. THE YOUTH WORKER'S ROLE IN CHANGING STEREOTYPED PATTERNS OF
      EXPECTATION
   D. THE DESIRABILITY OF INTERACTION PATTERNS

6.____

7. According to the above paragraph, a youth who misbehaves and is told by an agency
   worker that *his group is a menace to the community* would PROBABLY eventually
   respond by

   A. withdrawing into himself
   B. continuing to misbehave
   C. making a greater attempt to please
   D. acting indifferent

7.____

8. In the above paragraph, the author's opinion about stereotypes is that they are

8.____

A.   *useful,* primarily because they are usually accurate
B.   *useful,* primarily because they make a quick response easier
C.   *harmful,* primarily because the adult community will be less aware of delinquents as a group
D.   *harmful,* primarily because they influence behavior

Questions 9-15.

DIRECTIONS: Questions 9 through 15 are to be answered SOLELY on the basis of the information in the following passage.

Laws concerning juveniles make it clear that the function of the courts is to treat delinquents, not to punish them. Many years ago, children were detained in jails or police lockups along with adult offenders. Today, however, it is recognized that separate detention is important for the protection of the children. Detention is now regarded as part of the treatment process.

Detention is not an ordinary child care job. On the one hand, it must be distinguished from mere shelter care, which is a custodial program for children whose families cannot care for them adequately. On the other hand, it must be distinguished from treatment in mental health institutions, which is meant for children who have very serious mental or psychological problems. The children in a detention facility are there because they have run into trouble with the law and because they must be kept in safe custody for a short period until the court decides the final action to be taken in each child's case.

The Advisory Committee on Detention and Shelter Care has outlined several basic objectives for a good detention service. One objective is secure custody. Like adults who are being detained until their cases come up before the court, children too will often want to escape from detention. Security measures must be adequate to prevent ordinary escape attempts, although at the same time a jail-like atmosphere should be avoided. Another objective is to provide constructive activities for the children and to give individual guidance through casework and group sessions. A final objective is to study each child individually so that useful information can be provided for court action and so that the mental, emotional, or other problems that have contributed to the child's difficulties can be identified.

9.   According to the above passage, laws concerning juveniles make it clear that the MAIN aim of the courts in handling young offenders is to _____ juvenile delinquents.   9._____

A.   punish
B.   provide treatment for
C.   relieve the families of
D.   counsel families which have

10.   The above passage IMPLIES that the former practice of locking up juveniles along with adults was   10._____

A.   *good* because it was more efficient than providing separate facilities
B.   *good* because children could then be protected by the adults
C.   *bad* because the children were not safe
D.   *bad* because delinquents need mental health treatment

11. The above passage says that a detention center differs from a shelter care facility in that   11.____
    the children in a detention center

    A. have been placed there permanently by their families or by the courts
    B. come from families who cannot or will not care for them
    C. have serious mental or psychological problems
    D. are in trouble with the law and must be kept in safe custody temporarily

12. The above passage mentions one specific way in which detained juveniles are like   12.____
    detained adults.
    This similarity is that both detained juveniles and detained adults

    A. may try to escape from the detention facility
    B. have been convicted of serious crimes
    C. usually come from bad family backgrounds
    D. have mental or emotional problems

13. The above passage lists several basic objectives that were outlined by the Advisory   13.____
    Committee on Detention and Child Care.
    Which one of the following aims is NOT given in the list of Advisory Committee objec-
    tives?

    A. Separating juvenile offenders from adult offenders
    B. Providing secure custody
    C. Giving individual guidance
    D. Providing useful information for court action

14. The above passage mentions a *custodial program*. This means MOST NEARLY   14.____

    A. janitor services
    B. a program to prevent jail escapes
    C. caretaking services for dependent children
    D. welfare payments to families with children

15. The above passage says that *security measures* are needed in a detention center PRI-   15.____
    MARILY in order to

    A. prevent unauthorized persons from entering
    B. prevent juveniles from escaping
    C. ensure that records are safeguarded for court action
    D. create a jail-like atmosphere

Questions 16-22.

DIRECTIONS: Questions 16 through 22 are to be answered SOLELY on the basis of the fol-
              lowing passage.

   Adolescents are among the last social groups in the world to be given the full nineteenth-
century colonial treatment. Our colonial administrators, at least at the higher policymaking
levels, are usually of the enlightened sort who decry the punitive expedition except as an
instrument of last resort, though they are inclined to tolerate a shade more brutality in the
actual school or police station than the law allows. They prefer, however, to study the young
with a view to understanding them, not for their own sake but in order to learn how to induce

them to abandon their barbarism and assimilate the folkways of normal adult life. The model emissary to the world of youth is no longer the tough disciplinarian but the trained youth worker, who works like a psychoanalytically oriented anthropologist. Like the best of missionaries, he is sent to work with, and is aware and critical of the larger society he represents. But fundamentally, he accepts it and often does not really question its basic value or its right to send him to wean the young from savagery.

The economic position of *the adolescent society,* like that of other colonies, is highly ambiguous. It is simultaneously a costly drain on the commonwealth and a vested interest of those members of the commonwealth who earn their living and their social role by exploiting it. Juvenile delinquency is destructive and wasteful, and efforts to control and combat it are expensive. Schooling is even more expensive. Both undertakings are justified on the assumption that youth must be drawn into the social order if the social order is to continue, and this is self-evident. But both act as agents of society as it now is, propagating social values and assumptions among a youth often cynical and distrustful but ignorant of the language or the moral judgments in terms of which social complaints might be couched. Neither the youth agency nor the school is usually competent or sufficiently independent to help adolescents examine the sources of their pain and conflict and think its meaning through, using their continuing experience of life to help them build better social arrangements in their turn. This, in a democracy, ought clearly to be among the most fundamental functions of citizenship education; in a public school system geared and responsive to local political demands and interests, it may well be impossible. Official agencies dealing with youth vary enormously in the pretexts and techniques with which they approach their clientele, from those of the young worker attached to a conflict gang to those of the citizenship education teacher in the academic track of a suburban high school. But they all begin, like a Colonial Office, with the assumption that the long-term interests of their clientele are consistent with the present interests of their sponsor.

16. The clientele and sponsor of official agencies dealing with youth are the   16._____

     A.   young and the adult   B.   young and the educators
     C.   educators and the young   D.   adult and the middle class

17. The author believes that the adolescent society is   17._____

     A.   a drain on the commonwealth from which almost no one benefits
     B.   the mainstay of the economy
     C.   mercilessly exploited by certain adults
     D.   costly to the government but a financial boon to certain adults

18. The author feels that society's present attempts to assimilate youth are motivated by   18._____

     A.   greed
     B.   a desire to end juvenile delinquency
     C.   a desire to maintain the status quo
     D.   a desire to induce the young to abandon their barbarism

19. The author is _____ society and _____ of youth.   19._____

     A.   *approving* of present day; disapproving
     B.   *approving* of present day; approving
     C.   *disapproving* of adult; disapproving
     D.   *disapproving* of adult; approving

20. According to the above passage, the BASIC function of citizenship education in a democracy ought to be to

    20.____

    A. help adolescents examine the source of their pain and conflict
    B. help adolescents think the meaning of their problems through
    C. enable adolescents to perceive the meaning of experience
    D. enable adolescents to improve society through an understanding of their problems

21. The author is LEAST critical of

    21.____

    A. nineteenth-century Colonialists
    B. the trained youth worker
    C. the members of the commonwealth who earn their living exploiting youth
    D. official agencies dealing with youth

22. It is implied in the above passage that

    22.____

    A. colonialism is beneficial to the colonies
    B. society should not be stagnant but needs change
    C. society should have more effective ways of disciplining recidivists
    D. youth is more interested in track than citizenship education

Question 23.

DIRECTIONS: Question 23 is to be answered SOLELY on the basis of the following passage.

    Some adolescents find it very difficult to take the first step toward independence. Instead of experimenting as his friends do, a teenager may stay close to home, conforming to his parents' wishes. Sometimes parents and school authorities regard this untroublesome youngster with satisfaction and admiration, but they are wrong to do so. A too-conforming adolescent will not develop into an independent adult.

23. The above passage implies that a teenager who always conforms to his parents' wishes

    23.____

    A. should be admired by his teachers
    B. will develop into a troublesome person
    C. will become very independent
    D. should be encouraged to act more independently

Questions 24-25.

DIRECTIONS: Questions 24 and 25 are to be answered SOLELY on the basis of the following paragraph.

    The skilled children's counselor can encourage the handicapped child to make a maximum adjustment to the demands of learning and socialization. She will be aware that the child's needs are basically the same as those of other children and yet she will be sensitive to his special needs and the ways in which these are met. She will understand the frustration the child may experience when he cannot participate in the simple activities of childhood. She will also be aware of the need to help him to avoid repeated failures by encouraging him to engage in projects in which he can generally succeed and perhaps excel.

24. According to the above paragraph, it is important for the children's counselor to realize that the handicapped child   24.____

    A. should not participate in ordinary activities
    B. must not be treated in any special way
    C. is sensitive to the counselor's problems
    D. has needs similar to those of other children

25. According to the above paragraph, the counselor can BEST help the handicapped child to avoid frustrating situations by encouraging him to   25.____

    A. participate in the same activities as *normal* children
    B. participate in activities which are not too difficult for him
    C. engage in projects which are interesting
    D. excel in difficult games

KEY (CORRECT ANSWERS)

1.	D		11.	D
2.	C		12.	A
3.	A		13.	A
4.	B		14.	C
5.	C		15.	B
6.	C		16.	A
7.	B		17.	D
8.	D		18.	C
9.	B		19.	D
10.	C		20.	D

21.	B
22.	B
23.	D
24.	D
25.	B

REPORT WRITING
EXAMINATION SECTION
TEST 1

DIRECTIONS: Each question or incomplete statement is followed by several suggested answers or completions. Select the one that BEST answers the question or completes the statement. *PRINT THE LETTER OF THE CORRECT ANSWER IN THE SPACE AT THE RIGHT.*

Questions 1-3.

DIRECTIONS: Questions 1 to 3 are based on the following example of a report. The report consists of ten numbered sentences, some of which are *not* consistent with the principles of good report writing.

(1) On the evening of February 24, Roscoe and Leroy, two members of the "Red Devils," were entering with a bottle of wine in their hands. (2) It was unusually good wine for these boys to buy, (3) I told them to give me the bottle and they refused, and added that they wouldn"t let anyone "put them out." (4) I told them they were entitled to have a good time, but they could not do it the way they wanted; there were certain rules they had to observe, (5) At this point, Roscoe said he had seen me box at camp and suggested that Leroy not accept my offer. (6) Then I said firmly that the admission fee did not give them the authority to tell me what to do. (7) I also told them that, if they thought I would fight them over such a matter, they were sadly mistaken. (8) I added, however, that we could go to the gym right now and settle it another way if they wished. (9) Leroy immediately said that he was sorry, he had not understood the rules, and he did not want his quarter back. (10) On the other hand, they would not give up their bottle either, so they left the premises..

1. Only material that is relevant to the main thought of a report should be included. Which of the following sentences from the report contains material which is LEAST relevant to this report? Sentence

    A. 2   B. 3   C. 8   D. 9

2. A good report should be arranged in logical order. Which of the following sentences from the report does NOT appear in its proper sequence in the report? Sentence

    A. 3   B. 5   C. 7   D. 9

3. Reports should include all essential information.
    Of the following, the MOST important fact that is *missing* from this report is:

    A. Who was involved in the incident
    B. How the incident was resolved
    C. When the incident took place
    D. Where the incident took place

1.____

2.____

3.____

4. The MOST serious of the following faults *commonly* found in explanatory reports is   4.____

    A. the use of slang terms   B. excessive details
    C. C. personal bias   D. redundancy

5. In reviewing a report he has prepared to submit to his superiors, a supervisor finds that   5.____
his paragraphs are a typewritten page long and decides to make some revisions.
Of the following, the MOST important question he should ask about each paragraph
is:

    A. Are the words too lengthy?
    B. Is the idea under discussion too abstract?
    C. Is more than one central thought being expressed?
    D. Are the sentences too long?

6. The summary or findings of a long management report intended for the typical manager   6.____
should, *generally,* appear

    A. at the very beginning of the report
    B. at the end of the report
    C. throughout the report
    D. in the middle of the report

7. In preparing a report that includes several tables, if not otherwise instructed, the typist   7.____
should *most properly* include a list of tables

    A. in the introductory part of the report
    B. at the end of each chapter in the body of the report
    C. in the supplementary part of the report as an appendix
    D. in the supplementary part of the report as a part of the index

8. When typing a preliminary draft of a report, the one of the following which you should   8.____
generally NOT do is to

    A. erase typing errors and deletions rather than "X"ing them out
    B. leave plenty of room at the top, bottom and sides of each page
    C. make only the number of copies that you are asked to make
    D. type double or triple space

9. When you determine the methods of emphasis you will use in typing the titles, headings   9.____
and subheadings of a report, the one of the following which it is MOST important to keep
in mind is that

    A. all headings of the same rank should be typed in the same way
    B. all headings should be typed in the single style which is most pleasing to the eye
    C. headings should not take up more than one third of the page width
    D. only one method should be used for all headings, whatever their rank

10. The one of the following ways in which inter-office memoranda *differ* from long formal   10.____
reports is that they, *generally,*

    A. are written as if the reader is familiar with the vocabulary and technical background
of the writer
    B. do not have a "subject line" which describes the major topic covered in the text

    C.   include a listing of reference materials which support the memo writer's conclusions
    D.   require that a letter of transmittal be attached

11. It is *preferable* to print information on a field report rather than write it out longhand MAINLY because   11.____

    A.   printing takes less time to write than writing longhand
    B.   printing is usually easier to read than longhand writing
    C.   longhand writing on field reports is not acceptable in court cases
    D.   printing occupies less space on a report than longhand writing

12. Of the following characteristics of a written report, the one that is MOST important is its   12.____

    A.   length   B.   accuracy   C.   organization   D.   grammar

13. A written report to your superior contains many spelling errors.
Of the following statements relating to spelling errors, the one that is *most nearly* correct is that   13.____

    A.   this is unimportant as long as the meaning of the report is clear
    B.   readers of the report will ignore the many spelling errors
    C.   readers of the report will get a poor opinion of the writer of the report
    D.   spelling errors are unimportant as long as the grammar is correct

14. Written reports to your superior should have the same general arrangement and layout. The BEST reason for this requirement is that the   14.____

    A.   report will be more accurate
    B.   report will be more complete
    C.   person who reads the report will know what the subject of the report is
    D.   person who reads the report will know where to look for information in the report

15. The first paragraph of a report usually contains detailed information on the subject of the report.
Of the following, the BEST reason for this requirement is to enable the   15.____

    A.   reader to quickly find the subject of the report
    B.   typist to immediately determine the subject of the report so that she will understand what she is typing
    C.   clerk to determine to whom copies of the report shall be routed
    D.   typist to quickly determine how many copies of the report will be needed

16. Of the following statements concerning reports, the one which is LEAST valid is: 16.____

    A.   A case report should contain factual material to support conclusions made.
    B.   An extremely detailed report may be of less value than a brief report giving the essential facts.
    C.   Highly technical language should be avoided as far as possible in preparing a report to be used at a court trial.
    D.   The position of the important facts in a report does not influence the emphasis placed on them by the reader.

17. Suppose that you realize that you have made an error in a report that has been for-   17.____
warded to another unit. You know that this error is not likely to be discovered for some
time.
Of the following, the MOST advisable course of action for you to take is to

    A. approach the supervisor of the other unit on an informal basis, and ask him to cor-
rect the error
    B. say nothing about it since most likely one error will not invalidate the entire report
    C. tell your supervisor immediately that you have made an error so that it may be cor-
rected, if necessary
    D. wait until the error is discovered and then admit that you had made it

18. In a report, words in a sentence must be arranged properly to make sure that the   18.____
intended meaning of the sentence is clear.
The sentence below that does NOT make sense because a clause has been sepa-
rated from the word on which its meaning depends is:

    A. To be a good writer, clarity is necessary.
    B. To be a good writer, you must write clearly.
    C. You must write clearly to be a good writer.
    D. Clarity is necessary to good writing.

19. The use of a graph to show statistical data in a report is *superior* to a table because it   19.____

    A. emphasizes approximations
    B. emphasizes facts and relationships more dramatically
    C. presents data more accurately
    D. is easily understood by the average reader

20. Of the following, the degree of formality required of a written report is, *most likely* to   20.____
depend on the

    A. subject matter of the report
    B. frequency of its occurrence
    C. amount of time available for its preparation
    D. audience for whom the report is intended

Questions 21-25.

DIRECTIONS: Questions 21 through 25 consist of sets of four sentences lettered A, B, C, and
For each question, choose the sentence which is grammatically and stylisti-
cally *most appropriate* for use in a *formal* WRITTEN REPORT.

21.   A. It is recommended, therefore, that the impasse panelhearings are to be convened   21.____
on September 30.
    B. It is therefore recommended that the impasse panel hearings be convened on
September 30.
    C. Therefore, it is recommended to convene the impasse panel hearings on Sep-
tember 30.
    D. It is recommended that the impasse panel hearings therefore should be con-
vened on September 30.

22. A. Penalties have been assessed for violating the TaylorLaw by several unions.
    B. When they violated provisions of the Taylor Law, several unions were later penalized.
    C. Several unions have been penalized for violating provisions of the Taylor Law.
    D. Several unions' violating provisions of the Taylor Law resulted in them being penalized.

    22._____

23. A. The number of disputes settled through mediation has increased significantly over the past two years.
    B. The number of disputes settled through mediation are increasing significantly over two-year periods.
    C. Over the past two years, through mediation, the number of disputes settled increased significantly.
    D. There is a significant increase over the past two years of the number of disputes settled through mediation.

    23._____

24. A. The union members will vote to determine if the contract is to be approved.
    B. It is not yet known whether the union members will ratify the proposed contract.
    C. When the union members vote, that will determine the new contract.
    D. Whether the union members will ratify the proposed contract, it is not yet known.

    24._____

25. A. The parties agreed to an increase in fringe benefits in return for greater work productivity.
    B. Greater productivity was agreed to be provided in return for increased fringe benefits.
    C. Productivity and fringe benefits are interrelated; the higher the former, the more the latter grows.
    D. The contract now provides that the amount of fringe benefits will depend upon the level of output by the workers.

    25._____

———

KEY (CORRECT ANSWERS)

1.	A		11.	B
2.	B		12.	B
3.	D		13.	C
4.	C		14.	D
5.	C		15.	A
6.	A		16.	D
7.	A		17.	C
8.	A		18.	A
9.	A		19.	B
10.	A		20.	D

21. B
22. C
23. A
24. B
25. A

TEST 2

Questions 1-4.

DIRECTIONS: Answer Questions 1 through 4 on the basis of the following report which was prepared by a supervisor for inclusion in his agency's annual report.

Line #	
1	On Oct. 13, I was assigned to study the salaries paid
2	to clerical employees in various titles by the city and by
3	private industry in the area.
4	In order to get the data I needed, I called Mr. Johnson at
5	the Bureau of the Budget and the payroll officers at X Corp.—
6	a brokerage house, Y Co.—an insurance company, and Z Inc.—
7	a publishing firm. None of them was available and I had to call
8	all of them again the next day.
9	When I finally got the information I needed, I drew up a
10	chart, which is attached. Note that not all of the companies I
11	contacted employed people at all the different levels used in the
12	city service.
13	The conclusions I draw from analyzing this information is
14	as follows: The city's entry-level salary is about average for
15	the region; middle-level salaries are generally higher in the
16	city government than in private industry; but salaries at the
17	highest levels in private industry are better than city em-
18	ployees' pay.

1. Which of the following criticisms about the style in which this report is written is MOST valid?

   A. It is too informal.
   C. It is too choppy.
   B. It is too concise.
   D. The syntax is too complex.

2. Judging from the statements made in the report, the method followed by this employee in performing his research was

   A. *good;* he contacted a representative sample of businesses in the area
   B. *poor;* he should have drawn more definite conclusions
   C. *good;* he was persistent in collecting information
   D. *poor;* he did not make a thorough study

3. One sentence in this report contains a grammatical error. This sentence *begins* on line number

   A. 4   B. 7   C. 10   D. 13

4. The type of information given in this report which should be presented in footnotes or in an appendix, is the

    A.   purpose of the study
    B.   specifics about the businesses contacted
    C.   reference to the chart
    D.   conclusions drawn by the author

5.   Of the following, a DISTINGUISHING characteristic of a written report intended for the   5.____
    head of your agency as compared to a report prepared for a lower-echelon staff member
    is that the report for the agency head should, *usually,* include

    A.   considerably more detail, especially statistical data
    B.   the essential details in an abbreviated form
    C.   all available source material
    D.   an annotated bibliography

6.   Assume that you are asked to write a lengthy report for use by the administrator of your   6.____
    agency, the subject of which is "The Impact of Proposed New Data Processing Opera-
    tions on Line Personnel" in your agency. You decide that the *most appropriate* type of
    report for you to prepare is an analytical report, including recommendations.
    The MAIN reason for your decision is that

    A.   the subject of the report is extremely complex
    B.   large sums of money are involved
    C.   the report is being prepared for the administrator
    D.   you intend to include charts and graphs

7.   Assume that you are preparing a report based on a survey dealing with the attitudes of   7.____
    employees in Division X regarding proposed new changes in compensating employees
    for working overtime. Three percent of the respondents to the survey voluntarily offer an
    unfavorable opinion on the method of assigning overtime work, a question not speci-cally
    asked of the employees.
    On the basis of this information, the MOST appropriate and significant of the following
    comments for you to make in the report with regard to employees' attitudes on assign-
    ing overtime work is that

    A.   an insignificant percentage of employees dislike the method of assigning overtime
        work
    B.   three percent of the employees in Division X dislike the method of assigning over-
        time work
    C.   three percent of the sample selected for the survey voiced an unfavorable opinion
        on the method of assigning overtime work
    D.   some employees voluntarily voiced negative feelings about the method of assign-
        ing overtime work, making it impossible to determine the extent of this attitude

8.   Assume that you have been asked to prepare a narrative summary of the monthly   8.____
    reports submitted by employees in your division.
    In preparing your summary of this month's reports, the FIRST step to take is to

    A.   read through the reports, noting their general content and any unusual features
    B.   decide how many typewritten pages your summary should contain
    C.   make a written summary of each separate report, so that you will not have to go
        back to the original reports again
    D.   ask each employee which points he would prefer to see emphasized in your sum-
        mary

9. Assume that an administrative officer is writing a brief report to his superior outlining the advantages of matrix organization. Of the following, it would be INCORRECT to state that

    A. in matrix organization, a project is emphasized by designating one individual as the focal point for all matters pertaining to it
    B. utilization of manpower can be flexible in matrix organization because a reservoir of specialists is maintained in the line operations
    C. the usual line-staff management is generally reversed in matrix organization
    D. in matrix organization, responsiveness to project needs is generally faster due to establishing needed communication lines and decision points

9.____

10. Written reports dealing with inspections of work and installations SHOULD be

    A. as long and detailed as practicable
    B. phrased with personal interpretations
    C. limited to the important facts of the inspection
    D. technically phrased to create an impression on superiors

10.____

11. It is important to use definite, exact words in preparing a descriptive report and to avoid, as much as possible, nouns that have vague meanings and, possibly, a different meaning for the reader than for the author.
Which of the following sentences contains only nouns that are *definite* and *exact*?

    A. The free enterprise system should be vigorously encouraged in the United States.
    B. Arley Swopes climbed Mount Everest three times last year.
    C. Beauty is a characteristic of all the women at the party.
    D. Gil Noble asserts that he is a real democrat.

11.____

12. One way of shortening an unnecessarily long report is to reduce sentence length by eliminating the use of several words where a single one that does not alter the meaning will do.
Which of the following sentences CANNOT be shortened without losing some of its information content?

    A. After being polished, the steel ball bearings ran at maximum speed.
    B. After the close of the war, John Taylor was made the recipient of a pension.
    C. In this day and age, you can call anyone up on the telephone.
    D. She is attractive in appearance, but she is a rather selfish person.

12.____

13. Employees are required to submit written reports of all unusual occurrences promptly. The BEST reason for such promptness is that the

    A. report may be too long if made at one's convenience
    B. employee will not be so likely to forget to make the report
    C. report will tend to be more accurate as to facts
    D. employee is likely to make a better report under pressure

13.____

14. In making a report, it is poor practice to erase information on the report in order to make a change because

    A. there may be a question of what was changed and why it was changed
    B. you are likely to erase through the paper and tear the report

14.____

    C.   the report will no longer look neat and presentable
    D.   the duplicate copies will be smudged

15.   The one of the following which BEST describes a periodic report is that it   15._____

    A.   provides a record of accomplishments for a given time span and a comparison with similar time spans in the past
    B.   covers the progress made in a project that has been postponed
    C.   integrates, summarizes, and, perhaps, interprets published data on technical or scientific material
    D.   describes a decision, advocates a policy or action, and presents facts in support of the writer's position

16.   The PRIMARY purpose of including pictorial illustrations in a formal report is *usually* to   16._____

    A.   amplify information which has been adequately treated verbally
    B.   present details that are difficult to describe verbally
    C.   provide the reader with a pleasant, momentary distraction
    D.   present supplementary information incidental to the main ideas developed in the report

———

KEY (CORRECT ANSWERS)

1.	A		6.	A
2.	D		7.	D
3.	D		8.	A
4.	B		9.	C
5.	B		10.	C

11.	B
12.	A
13.	C
14.	A
15.	A
16.	B

———